uptospeed

Photoshop CS4

The only book
focused exclusively
on the new features
in Photoshop CS4

Ben Willmore

The Experts Agree...

"Ben is, without a doubt, one of the most gifted and talented Photoshop teachers on the planet, and this book is a brilliant way to learn the new features fast, in a way that only Ben can teach it. Highly recommended!"
–**Scott Kelby** Editor & Publisher, *Photoshop User Magazine* (PhotoshopUser.com)

"I don't read Photoshop books anymore, except one—Ben Willmore's Up to Speed. Even though many of us in the photographic community are members of the Photoshop development and beta teams, we still read this book. You don't need to read another thing. Ben is a force of Nature."
–**George DeWolfe** Senior Editor, *View Camera* and *Camera Arts Magazines* (GeorgeDeWolfe.com)

"Ben is no shill, he doesn't just tell you what's new and great... if he sees a weakness he's quick to point that out as well. If you want a comprehensive and easy to read update on the latest version of Photoshop, then Ben's book is the one for you."
–**Taz Tally** Author, *Avoiding the Output Blues* (TazSeminars.com)

"Ben has done it again! He has taken the voodoo out of the new release of CS4 and made it simple and easy to do more then just get up to speed. I depend on his book to make the new release a quick learn and usable tool in my workflow and teaching. He does not disappoint, his new book makes me look like a genius!"
–**Moose Peterson** Author 23 books and Nikon Legend Behind the Lens (MoosePeterson.com)

"The quickest way I get up to speed on EVERY new version of Photoshop is to talk Ben in to letting me read his Up To Speed books just before they go to press. I find them to be concise, to the point and explained in such a way that just makes sense. I wish every Photoshop book was written with the ease of Ben's books."
–**Vincent Versace** Author, *Welcome to OZ: A Cinematic Approach to Digital Photography* (VersacePhotography.com)

"Ben has once again saved me valuable time in getting going on the latest version of Photoshop. What I like most about Ben's way of addressing Photoshop is that he has become an excellent photographer, understands how photographers think and makes it all understandable and relatively simple. That's a pretty neat trick with all that Photoshop does!"
– **George D. Lepp** Field Editor, *Outdoor Photographer* and *PC Photo Magazines* (GeoLepp.com)

"Tastes Great - Less Filling!!! That's right, Ben delivers ALL the meat about what's new in CS4, with none of the wasted calories associated with wading through giant buffet-sized books! An absolute must-have! Don't hesitate. Without this book, you are wasting precious time, energy and money."

— *Jack Davis* Author of the *Photoshop Wow* and *How to Wow* series (AdventuresInPhotoshop.com)

"Ben's insights in his Up to Speed books always save me so much time. With Ben's help I can quickly learn the newest, most important features in Photoshop without having to wade through a lot of useless information. Ben delivers all I need in a comprehensive and easy to understand manner. Once again he delivers a book I can't live without!"

—*Lewis Kemper* Contributing Editor, *Outdoor Photographer* and *PC Photo Magazines* (LewisKemper.com)

"I have always enjoyed the way that Ben explains things. He makes even complex subjects seem easy. Add to this, his passion for the art and you have a book that not only informs but also inspires."

— *Colin Smith* Author or Co-Author of more than 15 books on Photoshop (PhotoshopCAFE.com)

"You've worked with Photoshop for years. You already know the program. You don't need a refresher course. You just need to know what's new. This book is for you!"

—*Pete Bauer* Author, *Photoshop for Dummies*

"One of the reasons I look forward to a new version of Photoshop is not necessarily in the program itself or the new bells and whistles as much as knowing that there will be a new UP TO SPEED book that will make all of the new stuff really rock for me. If you want to be the best at what you do, Ben's book is just for you."

—*Randy Hufford* Director of New Technology, *Institute Of Visual Arts Maui* (ivaMaui.com).

"A new version of Photoshop! What do all these new things do? Don't worry, Ben guides you through what is new in a way that makes the anxiety go away. Ben is the medicine for the headache of the upgrade transition."

— *Bert Monroy* Hyper-realistic Artist and Author *Photoshop Studio: Digital Painting* (BertMonroy.com)

Adobe Photoshop CS4: Up to Speed

Ben Willmore

Peachpit Press
1249 Eighth Street
Berkeley, CA 94710
(510) 524-2178
(510) 524-2221 (fax)
Find us on the World Wide Web at: http://www.peachpit.com
Peachpit Press is a division of Pearson Education

Copyright © 2009 by Ben Willmore
Cover design: Chris Klimek, Regina Cleveland, Ben Willmore
Book design: Ben Willmore
Project Editor: Wendy Sharp
Contributing Editor: Regina Cleveland
Production & Prepress: Ben Willmore, Hilal Sala
Direct-to-plate printing: Courier Printing

ISBN 13: 978-0-321-58005-4
ISBN 10: 0-321-58005-2

9 8 7 6 5 4 3 2 1

Printed and bound in the United States of America.

Photo Credits

All of the images in this book are copyrighted by Ben Willmore, with the following exceptions:

Cover Image
©2008 iStockphoto.com image:
Skier: #5664860/technotr

Design: Chris Klimek
Ben Willmore
Regina Cleveland

Chapter 1, Page 2
©2008 iStockphoto.com image:
Bridge: #1687380/Veni

Design: Regina Cleveland

Chapter 2, Page 26
©2008 iStockphoto.com image:
Woman: #878270/OneSureShot

Design: Regina Cleveland

Chapter 3, Page 38
©2008 iStockphoto.com images:
Bath: #902609/MilesSherrill
Cat: #5825274/SvetlanaGladkova
Monitor: #5272084/MorganLeFaye

Design: Regina Cleveland

Chapter 4, Page 48
©2008 iStockphoto.com images:
Dancer: #5857041/andyross
Curtains: #2633531/izusek

Design: Regina Cleveland

Chapter 5, Page 60
©2008 iStockphoto.com images:
House: #2972261/AlterYourReality
Spaceship: #182809/Redemption
Car: #953162/schlol,
Alien: #81812/LPETTET
Sky: #1089039/Romko_chuk

Design: Regina Cleveland

Chapter 6, Page 74
©2008 iStockphoto.com images:
Panorama: #2607034/narvikk
Parrot: #3212829/artzy
Hand: #2464084/markgoddard

Design: Regina Cleveland

Chapter 7, Page 100
©2008 iStockphoto.com images:
Multiple geishas: #1838318,
#1775338, #1775338/phfft
Fan: #742172/kingwahhaha
Umbrella: #2698524/Strauski
Cup: #1030414/jhason

Design: Regina Cleveland

Digital Mastery Ad
©2008 iStockphoto.com image:
Field of Heads: : #2419694/byllwill

Design: Regina Cleveland

Acknowledgements

I remember writing my very first seminar handbook. My editing team consisted of me, myself and the geek in the mirror. That was over a decade ago. Since then my adventures with Photoshop have put me in the path of some incredibly talented and gifted individuals, some of whom I wrangled into being a part of this book. They are:

The Queen—Regina Cleveland might as well be my outer cortex for she makes it possible for my gray matter to function properly. Had she not been a part of this project, it would have been like piloting a ship across the ocean with part of its hull missing. Regina makes it possible for me to concentrate on what's important because I know she'll handle all the details. She went way beyond the call of duty (as usual) tackling the chapter opener images as well as her usual role, which is to proof and edit every word I write.

The Peachpitters—Nancy Ruenzel, for enthusiastically supporting my idea for this book. When it comes to publishers, she's a swan in a sea of pigeons. Wendy Sharp, for her unwavering dedication to excellence and for mothering this project to its conclusion. Thanks also to Hilal Sala, our favorite production coordinator, and Rebecca Plunkett, our indexer.

The Brain Posse— Dan Burkholder and Jeff Tranberry (My Secret Weapon at Adobe) kindly took time out of their busy lives to review chapters and technical issues with a fine-tooth comb. They didn't just provide tech editing, they challenged me to write a better book.

The Artistes—Chris Klimek for coming up with the original cover design and Regina Cleveland for updating the cover for CS4 and for her delightful chapter openers.

The Mother Ship—John Nack and the folks at Adobe who pump out exciting new versions of Photoshop about every 18 months.

The Stock Broker—The good folks at iStockphoto.com for kindly letting us run loose in their wonderful image collections.

About The Author

A senior engineer from NASA once said that this man gave the best technical seminar he ever attended. That same year a computer-phobic who had been struggling with Photoshop for years proclaimed that "He takes the Boogie Man out of Photoshop!" This seems to be Ben Willmore's special gift; he has an uncanny ability to connect with users of every level and mind-set; whether it's first-timers taking their first sniff of Photoshop, or razor-sharp nerds and nerdettes who are on the fast track to technical enlightenment. The common echo that Ben leaves in his wake seems to be "Aha! I finally GET Photoshop!"

Considered to be one of the all-time great Photoshop gurus, Ben is one of those guys who zooms around the world standing in front of sellout crowds while he spreads his particular brand of illumination. To date, he has personally taught over 80,000 Photoshop users on five continents. His descriptions of Curves and Channels are thought to be the best in the industry and his breakthrough teaching style of "not-just-how-but-why," is what prompted the National Association of Photoshop Professionals to induct Ben into the Photoshop Hall of Fame in 2004.

His award-winning, best-selling book, *Photoshop Studio Techniques* is said to be "Arguably, one of the best Photoshop books ever written." by Photoshop User's publisher, Jim Workman.

Ben understands Photoshop on a genetic level. He grasps the underlying concepts no matter how difficult they seem to the rest of us, then presents them in a clear, understandable and most importantly useful way.
-Kevin Ames
Author, Digital Photographer's Notebook *(www.amesphoto.com)*

He continues to be a featured speaker at photography and publishing conferences and events worldwide, including Photoshop World, American Society of Media Photographers (ASMP), Professional Photographers Association (PPA) and the Royal Photographic Society of England. He's a member of the PhotoshopWorld Dream Team, is a PEI Photoshop All-Star, and writes for numerous digital imaging and photography publications, including a monthly column for *Photoshop User* magazine.

In 2006, Ben took his Photoshop adventures on the open road in a giant touring bus. His home/office-on-wheels has enabled him to rekindle his passion for photography and while many of us are hitting the snooze button, Ben is likely to be prowling around in the pre-dawn hours waiting for the perfect light. His road ramblings take him all over the United States, and if you're visiting a National Park this year, don't be surprised if you happen to see Ben toting his camera gear while he looks for his next inspiration; just be sure to get up early!

To see Ben's photos from the road, and to keep track of him while he is exploring America, visit: www.WhereIsBen.com.

Table of Contents

Introduction

Whenever Adobe churns out a new version of Photoshop, we find ourselves scrambling to learn the latest features. Each upgrade becomes more robust than the last, making the task of learning a daunting one. You can turn to books for help, but if it's just the new features you want, the books can be more intimidating than Photoshop because they're not designed to focus on the upgrade alone. Until now, Photoshop books could be grouped into one of three categories:

1) All encompassing 'bibles' that try to cover everything.

2) Cookbooks that present the reader with brief "recipe" techniques and no in-depth coverage.

3) Books that specialize in a particular area and are very in-depth (retouching, channels, color management, etc).

So, what's missing? There isn't one book out there that caters to the user who just wants in-depth coverage of the newest features of Photoshop. If you buy the bible type book, you'll likely waste a weekend with an often frustrating and time-consuming search through hundreds of pages. Ferreting out the new stuff with the specialist books is just as maddening because they only cover a fraction of the new features, and the recipe books just skim the surface, leaving you without any true understanding of the finer points that make Photoshop's features so powerful.

Up to Speed is the first book that cuts away the fat of what you already know about Photoshop and goes right to the new features. To make your knowledge upgrade as quick and effortless as possible, I include just enough information about older features so the new ones will make sense. And unlike the sales presentations or generic overviews that come out with every new release, this book presents all the features in my signature style: intuitive, crystal clear and in-depth; everything that you need to truly get "up to speed" with the new features of Photoshop.

Who Should Read This Book

You don't have to be an expert to benefit from this book. *Up to Speed* is for all users who have a working knowledge of Photoshop CS3. However, if you're not already comfortable with the CS3 version of Photoshop, this book might not be appropriate for you. If that's the case, I recommend you read my other book, *Photoshop Studio Techniques*, which covers the most important features in Photoshop, both old and new.

How It's Organized

Each chapter is organized so that you can quickly glance at the first page to get a good sense of what the chapter will cover. On the first page of each chapter you'll see a section called, "Where's My Stuff?" When Adobe moves things around, it can mess with your head, so this section tells you what to need to know about features that have either been changed, moved or eliminated to avoid getting upgrade vertigo when you start using CS4.

Keyboard commands are displayed for both Mac and Windows operating systems. Screenshots are from a Mac OS X system, but if you're a Windows user, don't worry, because even though they are cosmetically different, all the tools, palettes, menus, and dialog boxes are functionally identical.

What's Missing

Version Cue (the version management software that comes with the entire Creative Suite) is not covered here because it is beyond the objective of this book, which is to get you up to speed with Photoshop's newest features as quickly and smoothly as possible.

Also, since the introduction of CS3, Photoshop comes in two flavors—regular and extended. The Extended version includes all the features of regular Photoshop CS4, plus more. "More" includes a number of features designed for more technical users (engineers, scientists, medical professionals, architects, television/film folks, etc.). They include measurement and image analysis tools, the ability to edit 3D and motion based content, and tools for medical imaging, to mention a few. This book is intended for photographers and graphic designers (which is my area of expertise), so I won't be covering the Extended features.

The Lowdown on CS4

This upgrade is clear evidence of Adobe's determination to keep their eye on the distant horizon. Many of the new capabilities in CS4 represent the firstborn of a new generation of features that are a part of Adobe's long term grand plan to "dramatically redefine" Photoshop.

There is, of course, much to delight the user in CS4, but beyond what's visible to the naked eye, a fundamental shift in the underlying architecture of Photoshop has taken place under the hood. This primal shift is what has enabled Adobe to provide us with an experience that feels less constrained by gravitational pull, and closer to what might be described as a kind of buoyancy.

Much of this sensation of feeling released from Photoshop's shackles has to do with two of my favorite features in CS4, the new **Adjustments** and **Masks** panels. They are notable because they represent a giant step away from modal-style dialog boxes. A modal-style dialog box pops up, and while open you cannot access any other operation inside the application. This effectively puts you into a straight-jacket because, as all Photoshop users know, when any dialog box is open, there are always associated tasks that need attention at the same time, but those tasks must wait until you conclude your business in the dialog box. While there are still a good number of old-style dialog boxes populating Photoshop, these new-style panels are truly liberating because they allow you to do virtually anything else in Photoshop even while the panels are open.

Other new features that contribute to this sense of weightlessness are the new **Rotate View** tool (no more having to cock your head in painful angles), the flick-panning and animated zoom features (which make the navigation experience feel more like you're flying through the air instead of dodging cars on a busy street), and Bridge's new **Review** mode, which allows you to sift though your images as if they were floating in space.

In keeping with the same emancipation theme, Camera Raw 5.0 now includes a feature—the new **Adjustment** brush—that make it less essential than ever to venture into Photoshop. This single feature alone introduces an unprecedented level of control and flexibility to adjustments made in Camera Raw.

Of course there are heaps of other new goodies; Photoshop's new browser-style tabbed window option is awesome when working with multiple documents, and the new Flash panel capability is truly a window into the future. I think it's safe to say that nearly all the enhancements offered in CS4 will be greatly appreciated by the majority of Photoshop users.

While you're wandering through the maze of new features, take a moment to remember that Adobe often gives us more than at first meets the eye. That's why you'll want make sure to take the time to read through every chapter of this book (even if you've been using CS4 for awhile), because there's nothing better than getting a good surprise and hearing yourself say, "I didn't know CS4 did that!"

—Ben Willmore

Chapter 1
Bridge CS4

L IKE WATCHING A GANGLY TEENAGER mature into a full-size adult in slow-motion, so goes witnessing the evolution of Bridge. This latest upgrade is more about polishing and refinement than about whopping change. For some, the most dramatic events were the banishment of Adobe Stock Photos and the Photographers Directory.

Below is an overview of what we'll be covering in this chapter:

- **Interface Changes:** Re-orient yourself to the new surroundings by taking the all-inclusive Ben Willmore tour of Bridge CS4's redesigned interface.
- **Path Bar:** See how the second row of icons at the top of the Bridge window can help you navigate, sort and modify your images.
- **Collections Panel:** Learn how to organize your images into virtual collections without moving the files on your hard drive. This new panel replaces the Save as Collection button in the Find feature of Bridge CS3.
- **Output Panel:** Quickly create PDF documents and Web galleries with a panel full of options and templates that make it easier than ever to output to these formats.
- **Misc. Changes:** Discover how the smaller, less noticeable features can make a big difference in how you work with Bridge. You'll be introduced to the new View options, Load Files into Layers command, and for you touchy-feely folks, there is gesture support for multi-finger navigation in Bridge and slideshows.

Where's My Stuff?

It might take you a while to get your bearings with Bridge CS4. Adobe is working hard to modernize the underpinnings that hold Photoshop together, and as part of the new scheme a few major features have been removed without direct replacement. Read through this section to see what's what with your old favorites:

- **The Interface:** The background at the top and bottom of the window has been darkened. If you find it displeasing you can simply go to Bridge Preferences and adjust the **Appearance** sliders to your liking.
- **Adobe Stock Photos:** This feature has been discontinued. Professional photographers hated it because they felt it provided direct competition, while graphic designers loved the ability to search for photos without leaving Bridge. Whatever you thought about it, it's gone for good so if you need a replacement service try **iStockphoto.com**.
- **Adobe Photographers Directory:** Adobe has removed this feature from Bridge CS4.If you need an alternative, go to **ppa.com** and click their **Find a Photographer** link.

- **Favorites Pop-up Menu:** The **Favorites** pop-up menu that used to be found in the upper left of the Bridge window has been replaced by the down-pointing arrow icon that is found in about the same position.
- **Go Up One Folder Icon:** In CS3, clicking the **Go Up One Folder** icon would bring you one level up in the folder hierarchy. You can now do that by choosing the first choice listed in the same down-pointing arrow icon mentioned above, or by clicking one level back in the new Path bar that's found in the upper left of the Bridge window.

- **Include Subfolders Icon:** This icon was found in the Filter pane of Bridge CS3. There is no longer an icon that performs its function, but you can choose **Show Items from Subfolders** from the **View** menu, or by clicking the right-pointing arrow "**>**" at the end of the path and choosing **Show Items from Subfolders**.
- **Workspace Icons:** The four icons that were located in the lower right corner of the Bridge window have been replaced by the Workspace strip that is found just to the left of the Search field at the top of the Bridge window.

- **Accent Color:** Bridge CS3 used the same highlight color (now called accent color) as your operating system. In CS4 there is a new default, but you can change it back to the **System** setting in Bridge's **Preferences** dialog box.
- **Contact Sheet II:** This feature has been replaced by the new **Output** panel in CS4 (more on the Output panel coming up), and the only file format for a contact sheet is PDF (as opposed to multiple formats that were available in Photoshop). If you prefer the functionality from the previous version, feel free to copy the old plug-in from the **Photoshop CS3/**

Plug-ins/Automate folder into the same folder in Photoshop CS4. To use the command, you'll have to access it from the **File>Automate** menu in Photoshop.
- **PDF Presentation:** This feature was also wrapped into the new **Output** panel. Either use the **Output** panel as a replacement or copy the old filter to the appropriate folder in CS4.
- **Web Photo Gallery:** This is yet another feature that's been replaced by the **Output** panel, but the old version can be resurrected as mentioned above.
- **Picture Package:** There isn't an equivalent feature in Bridge CS4, but like the last few features, you can copy the old plug-in to restore that functionality.
- **Thumbnail Preference:** Some of the preferences for thumbnail generation have been replaced with two checkerboard icons that appear in the Path bar near the top of the Bridge window.
- **Preference Camera Raw:** Bridge used to feature a preference for how to handle opening JPEG and TIFF with Adobe Camera Raw. Those settings have been replaced with similar ones in the Camera Raw **Preferences** dialog box which can be accessed under the **Adobe Bridge CS4** menu (Mac), or **Edit** menu (Win).
- **High Quality Previews Preferences:** This option used to be found in the Advanced Preferences section and has been replaced by the same two checkerboard icons mentioned above.
- **Auto-launch Bridge:** The **Automatically Launch Bridge** setting that was previously found in the General Section of Photoshop's **Preferences** dialog box has been renamed **Start Bridge at Login** and has been moved to the Advanced section of Bridge's Preferences dialog box.
- **Generate Thumbnails Option:** The **High Quality** and **Quick Thumbnail** settings found under **Edit** menu have been replaced by the same two checkerboard icons mentioned above.
- **Start Meeting:** The features related to Acrobat Connect meetings have been removed from Bridge CS4. You can still access them through your web browser at **www.adobe.com/products/acrobatconnect/**

Adobe Bridge CS3 featured a brighter interface and fewer "gadgets" at the top of the window.

In Adobe Bridge CS4, quite a few things have been repositioned, redesigned or removed.

Interface Changes

The majority of interface changes can be seen at the top of the Bridge window. That's where you'll find a new row of icons along with a few workspace presets and the new search field. Let's explore this first row of icons before we move on to other areas of Bridge.

Quick Navigation Icons

You'll find the quick navigation icons (I made that term up because Adobe has yet to come up with a name) in the upper left of the Bridge window just to the right of the **Bridge** icon (which has no purpose other than to remind you of which program you're using).

Back & Forward Icons

The **left** and **right arrow** icons work in the same way as the ones that were found in Bridge CS3. These icons are similar to what you'll find in any web browser, taking you back or forward within the folders you've recently browsed.

Favorites Pop-up Menu

Clicking on the **down pointing arrow** icon that appears to the right of the **Back** and **Forward** icons will reveal the **Favorites** pop-up menu.

The top half of the menu lists the navigation path needed to get to the folder you are currently viewing. Clicking on any of the choices in that part of the menu will take you up one or more levels on your hard drive. This is the same information that you'll find in the **Path Bar** that we'll talk about later in this chapter.

The bottom half of the **Favorites** menu allows you to quickly navigate to any folders you've added to your favorites. To add a folder to your favorites, navigate to the folder within Bridge and then choose **Add to Favorites** from the **File** menu. This toggles to **Remove from Favorites** if you have previously defined it as a favorite. You can also add common locations to your favorites (such as the Desktop) by choosing among the settings available in the **General** section of the **Preferences** dialog box which is found under the **Adobe Bridge CS4** menu (Mac), or **Edit** menu (Win).

Recents Pop-up Menu

You'll find the **Recents** pop-up menu (which looks like the face of a clock) to the right of the **Favorites** menu.

Recent Folders: The **Recents** menu allows you to quickly navigate to folders you've recently visited. There is a setting in the **General** section of the **Preferences** dialog box that will determine how many folders Photoshop will keep track of (the default is 10).

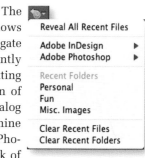

Recent Documents: In addition to keeping track of folders, Bridge CS4 also keeps track of documents you've opened in all the Creative Suite applications. These documents can be accessed via the submenus that appear near the top of the **Recents** menu (in the example above, I only have Photoshop and InDesign loaded on my computer). Choosing a document from one of the side menus will not actually open the file, but will instead cause Bridge to navigate to the folder that contains the document and highlight the file.

Reveal Files: The **Reveal All Recent Files** choice will cause Bridge to locate all the Creative Suite documents you've recently opened and display them in a virtual folder. You'll also find a **Recent Files** choice in each of the application-specific subfolders of the **Recents** menu, which will allow you to view files you've recently opened in their native Creative Suite applications.

NOTE

*The **Reveal Files** feature is taking advantage of a new feature in Bridge that is known as a **Collection**. We'll discuss **Collections** in detail later in this chapter.*

The **Clear Recent Folders** and **Clear Recent Files** choices will clear out the list of recent files or folders that are listed in the **Recents** menu. This is useful if you've been working with personal files and don't want your boss to easily find out that you've been less than, shall we say...productive? (We all do it, but never want to get caught.) A less under-handed and perhaps more constructive use for this feature would be when you have closed out a major project, are starting to work on a new one, and don't want the old stuff to clutter up the results of your Recent Files displays.

Adobe Photo Downloader

The icon that looks like a camera with a small down-pointing arrow next to it allows you to quickly access the **Adobe Photo Downloader**. The downloader is not new—it's only the icon that is new, which makes it much faster to access this feature compared to having to choose **Get Photos from Camera** from the **File** menu (which is how we did it in CS3). The Photo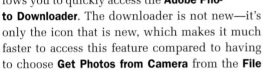

The CS4 Adobe Photo Downloader dialog box.

Downloader is designed to allow you to quickly download photographs from any attached digital camera or storage card.

There is only one new feature to be found in the **Photo Downloader** dialog box. The new **Delete Original Files** checkbox will delete the photos off the storage media after the images have been successfully copied. This helps to prevent you from downloading images twice, which is common if you forget to format your storage card before taking additional shots.

Refine Pop-up Menu

The **Refine** pop-up menu offers three choices, one that's new and two that have relocated from CS3.

Review Mode

This brand new mode provides a wonderfully clean, clutter-free background and enables you to quickly examine and sift though your images as if they were floating in air. It makes it especially easy to narrow down a large number of images to the select few that might be worth working on. You can access this mode by clicking its submenu name or typing **Command-B** (Mac), or **Ctrl-B** (Win). When four or fewer images are selected, the images will be shown side by side. When more than four images are selected, they will be shown in a carousel mode where only the front-most image is enlarged. You can press the **Right** and **Left Arrow** icons (or use their keyboard equivalents) to cycle through the images being shown, or click on any of the images with your mouse button which will immediately place it in the enlarged, front position. Whenever you run into an image that does not meet your quality standards (maybe it's out of focus or simply doesn't have a compelling composition) press the **Down Arrow** key (or click the **Down Arrow** icon) to remove it from the group of images.

Review mode presents you with a cascade of images. Press the down arrow key to remove an image from the review.

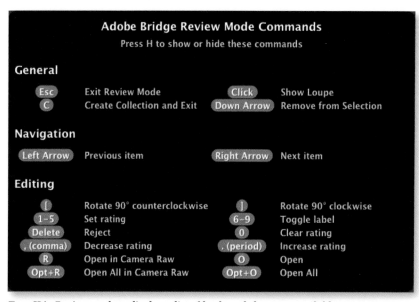

Type H in Review mode to display a list of keyboard shortcuts available.

 The new Collection (left) and Return to Bridge icons (right).

If you need to look at a portion of an image at 100% view, click the mouse button on the area (of the front position image) you'd like to magnify. You can also hold **Command** (Mac), or **Ctrl** (Win) and press the **Plus** or **Minus** keys to change the magnification.

Using keyboard shortcuts, you can rate each image, rotate them and more. To see all the available shortcuts, press the **H** key while in Review mode.

Once you've narrowed your selection of images, either click the **X** icon (or press the **Esc** key) to return to Bridge where the surviving images will be selected, or click the **Collection** icon to create a new Collection that contains the surviving images.

Batch Rename

The Batch Rename command is not new to Bridge CS4; it's just been added to the **Refine** pop-up menu. You can also choose the command from the **Tools** menu (just as you could in Bridge CS3). There are no new options in this feature, so let's move on.

File Info

The **File Info** dialog box is not new—it's been available from the **File** menu in Bridge and Photoshop for quite a few versions—but Adobe did add some nice little features to this dialog box, so let's take a look at what they've cooked up.

The old version of the dialog box had a fixed size that caused Adobe to separate a lot of related information into different sections. In Bridge CS4 (and Photoshop for that matter), they've made the dialog box re-sizable and consolidated many of the sections. For instance, the sections for IPTC Contact, IPTC Image, IPTC Content and

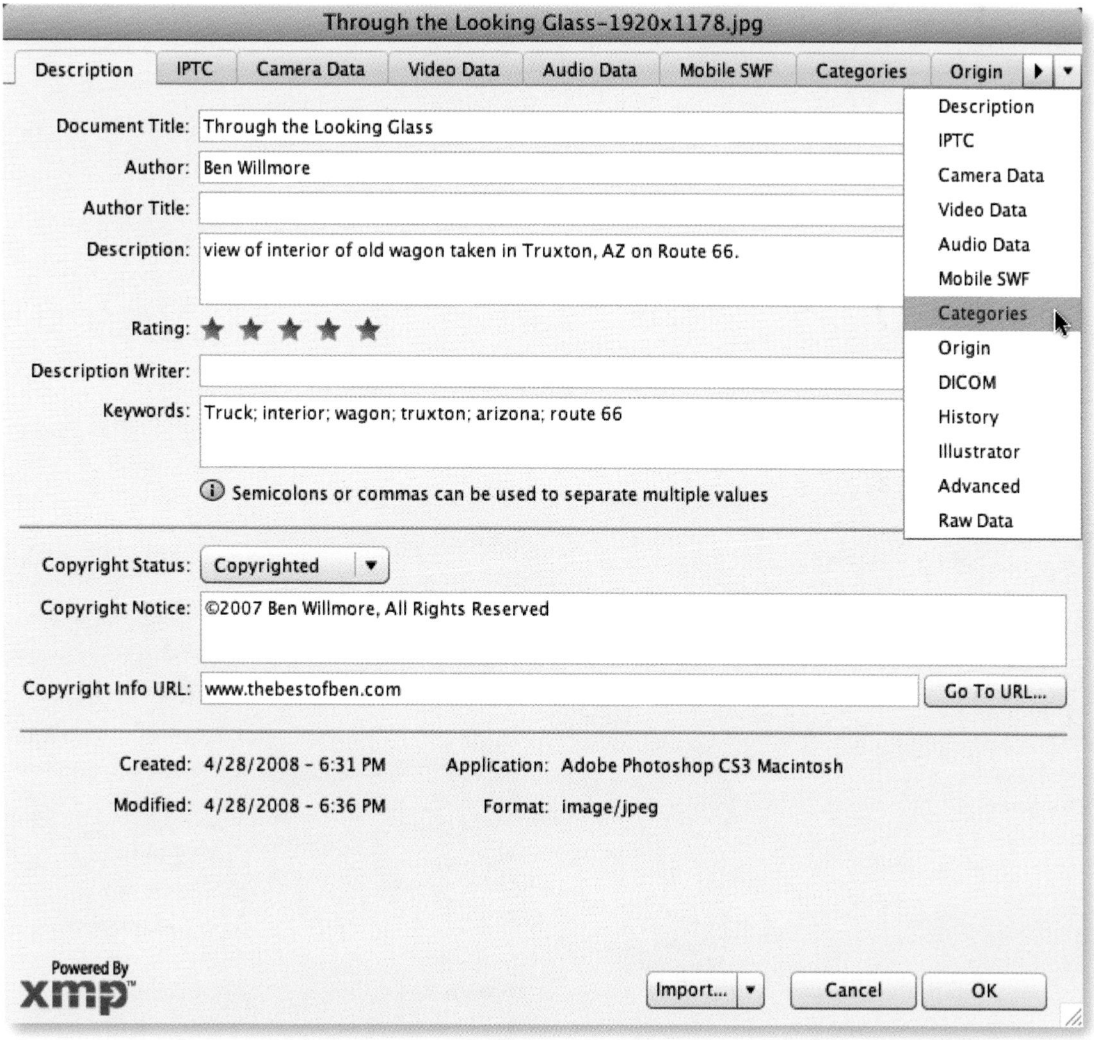

Through the Looking Glass-1920x1178.jpg

| Description | IPTC | Camera Data | Video Data | Audio Data | Mobile SWF | Categories | Origin | ▶ | ▼ |

Description
IPTC
Camera Data
Video Data
Audio Data
Mobile SWF
Categories
Origin
DICOM
History
Illustrator
Advanced
Raw Data

Document Title: Through the Looking Glass

Author: Ben Willmore

Author Title:

Description: view of interior of old wagon taken in Truxton, AZ on Route 66.

Rating: ★ ★ ★ ★ ★

Description Writer:

Keywords: Truck; interior; wagon; truxton; arizona; route 66

ⓘ Semicolons or commas can be used to separate multiple values

Copyright Status: Copyrighted ▼

Copyright Notice: ©2007 Ben Willmore, All Rights Reserved

Copyright Info URL: www.thebestofben.com   Go To URL...

Created: 4/28/2008 - 6:31 PM   Application: Adobe Photoshop CS3 Macintosh

Modified: 4/28/2008 - 6:36 PM   Format: image/jpeg

Powered By
xmp™

Import... ▼   Cancel   OK

The File Info dialog box in Bridge CS4 has been redesigned.

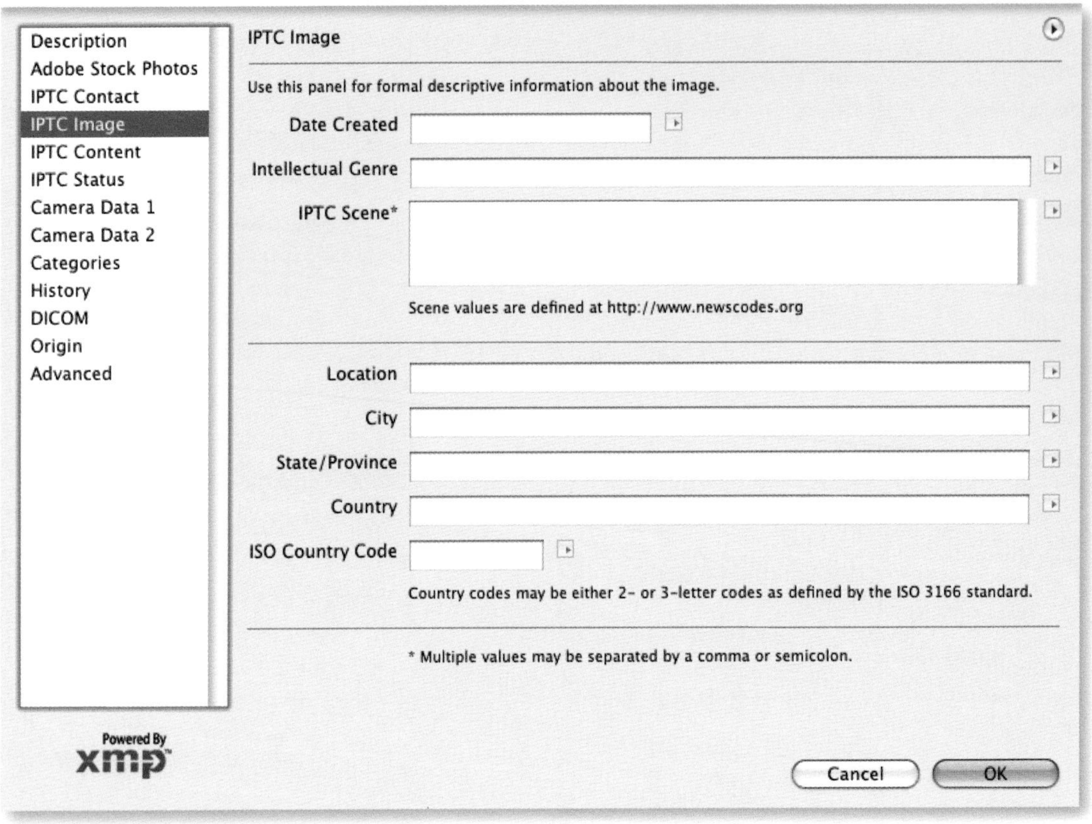

Description	IPTC Image	
Adobe Stock Photos		
IPTC Contact	Use this panel for formal descriptive information about the image.	

Description
Adobe Stock Photos
IPTC Contact
IPTC Image
IPTC Content
IPTC Status
Camera Data 1
Camera Data 2
Categories
History
DICOM
Origin
Advanced

IPTC Image

Use this panel for formal descriptive information about the image.

Date Created

Intellectual Genre

IPTC Scene*

Scene values are defined at http://www.newscodes.org

Location

City

State/Province

Country

ISO Country Code

Country codes may be either 2- or 3-letter codes as defined by the ISO 3166 standard.

* Multiple values may be separated by a comma or semicolon.

Powered By
xmp

Cancel   OK

The CS3 version of the File Info dialog box.

IPTC Status have been combined into a single tab that contains all the IPTC info. At the same time, they added new categories for **Video Data**, **Audio Data**, **Mobile SWF** (SWF is the file format for Adobe Flash content) and **Illustrator**.

The redesigned dialog box displays the file info categories in tabs across the top of the dialog box (type **Command-Arrow** on the Mac or **Ctrl-Arrow** on Windows to cycle through the tabs). If the dialog box is not wide enough to show all the tabs, you can click on the arrow icons found on either end of the tab bar. Or, if you don't feel like arrowing

NOTE

What's the IPTC?

IPTC is an acronym for the International Press Telecommunications Council. The IPTC is a consortium of over 70 of the world's major news agencies that was formed to come up with standard ways of attaching text that describes an image to the image itself.

your way to the tab you desire, you can choose from the drop down menu in the upper right corner of the dialog box.

You can remove tabs from the File Info dialog box by removing the corresponding folder from the following directory on your hard drive:

Mac: HD: Library: Application Support: Adobe: XMP: Custom File Info Panels: 2.0: panels

Windows: C:\ Program Files\ Common Files\ Adobe \XMP\ Custom File Info Panels\ 2.0\ panels

If you look at the screen shots of each of the new tabs you will quickly get an idea of what type of metadata they were designed to contain.

They only major changes to the existing metadata categories are the addition of a 1-5 star rating in the Description tab and various calendar icons in areas where you can enter a date.

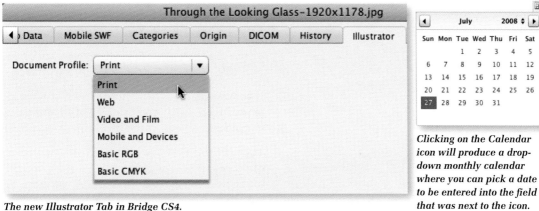

Through the Looking Glass-1920x1178.jpg

| Description | IPTC | Camera Data | Video Data | Audio Data | Mobile SWF | Categories | Origin | ▶ | ▼ |

Title: Through the Looking Glass

Artist:

Album:

Track Number:

Genre:

Composer:

Engineer:

Release Date:

Creation Date: 4/28/2008 6:31 PM

Copyright: ©2007 Ben Willmore, All Rights Reserved

Software Package: Adobe Photoshop CS3 Macintosh

Comments:

Sample Rate:

Bit Rate:

Channels:

Duration:

BWF Time Reference:

Format:

Powered By
xmp

Import... ▼   Cancel   OK

The new Audio Data Tab in Bridge CS4.

Through the Looking Glass-1920x1178.jpg

| ◀ Data | Mobile SWF | Categories | Origin | DICOM | History | Illustrator |

Document Profile: Print ▼

Print
Web
Video and Film
Mobile and Devices
Basic RGB
Basic CMYK

◀ July 2008 ⬍ ▶

Sun	Mon	Tue	Wed	Thu	Fri	Sat
		1	2	3	4	5
6	7	8	9	10	11	12
13	14	15	16	17	18	19
20	21	22	23	24	25	26
27	28	29	30	31		

Clicking on the Calendar icon will produce a drop-down monthly calendar where you can pick a date to be entered into the field that was next to the icon.

The new Illustrator Tab in Bridge CS4.

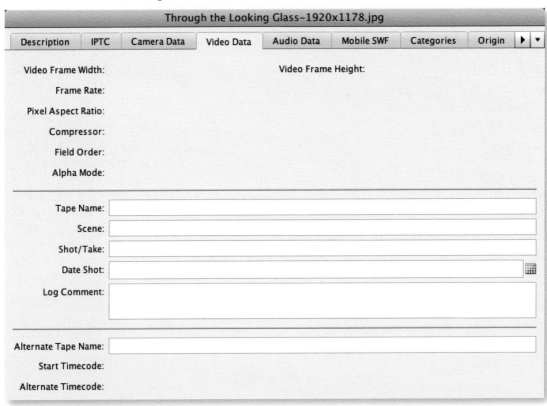

The new Mobile SWF Tab in Bridge CS4.

The new Video Data Tab in Bridge CS4.

Open In Camera Raw

The new **Open in Camera Raw** icon is just a shortcut for choosing the same command under the **File** menu. This icon doesn't allow you to do anything that couldn't be done in earlier versions of the program. If the icon ever appears to be dark gray instead of light gray, it's an indication that the file you have selected is not compatible with Camera Raw. The most common culprit would be a TIFF file that contains layers. Camera Raw can only open flattened RAW, JPEG and TIFF images.

Output Menu

The **Output** pop-up menu is a little odd in that it only features one choice and therefore would have been more appropriately implemented as an icon instead of a menu. Choosing **Output to Web or PDF** will open the new **Output** panel, which we'll discuss later in this chapter.

Workspaces

You'll find the new Workspace strip near the upper right of the Bridge window. You can change the size of the strip by dragging on the grabber bar that appears on its left edge.

Workspaces are presets that can change which panels (also known as palettes) are visible, where they are located on screen, as well as which menu items are visible and the keyboard shortcuts assigned to each menu item. Workspaces are not new to CS4, but the new Workspace strip makes it easier than ever to switch between them.

Adobe has also changed some of the default Workspaces and introduced a few new ones. None of this is ground breaking since you can always create your own Workspace by arranging the panels the way you please and then choosing New Workspace from the pop-up menu that appears on the right edge of the Workspace strip.

Search Field

A new Search field has been added to the upper right of the Bridge window. This field not only uses Bridge's built-in search capabilities, it can also access your operating system's global search features (Spotlight on the Mac and Windows Desktop on Windows).

Clicking on the arrow next to the Search icon allows you to choose which search engine you'd like to use and gives you quick access to recent searches (Draft and Final in this example). While this feature is a great addition to Bridge, it's lacking somewhat in that it doesn't offer any refinement options for you to narrow your search prior to performing the search. For instance you can't perform a search for files with a name that contains or begins/ends with the string you typed in the search field (for that type of search you're still better off using the **Edit>Find** command). As it stands now you get all the files that not only contain the string in its filename, but in its contents (including metadata) as well. You can use the **Sort** drop-down menu (directly below the **Search** field) to organize your search results, but it still casts too large of a net and you can end up looking at hundreds of files that have nothing to do with what you are searching for. Hopefully Adobe will add those refinements in the future which would make this new Search feature much more powerful.

When the thumbnail grid is unlocked, thumbnail images are allowed to scroll partially out of view.

Locking the thumbnail grid prevents thumbnail images from being cut off at the top or bottom of the window.

View Icons

At the bottom right of the Bridge window you'll find  four new icons. From left to right, the icons are **Lock Thumbnail Grid**, **View as Thumbnails**, **View as Details**, **View as List**.

Lock Thumbnail Grid: This feature prevents thumbnail images from being cut off at the top or bottom of the Bridge window. That way you can use the **Up** or **Down Arrow** keys to scroll through your images without having to see any partial thumbnails.

View as Thumbnails: Displays your images as thumbnail images with the name and rating shown below.

View as Details: Displays a thumbnail on the far left with basic metadata filling the right side of your screen.

View as List: Displays a small thumbnail for each image and a single line of metadata. You can quickly sort the images by clicking on the headings at the top of each column of metadata. **Control-click** (Mac) or **Right-click** (Win) on the headings to access a menu allowing you to change which metadata will be displayed.

Path Bar

The second row of icons near the top of the Bridge window is known as the Path bar.

File Path Hierarchy

On the left side, it contains a breadcrumb-style path that indicates how you'd have to navigate to get to the folder you're currently viewing. You can click on any of the folders within the path to instantly move to that location.

Thumbnail Quality Icons

To the right of the Path Hierarchy, you'll find two Thumbnail Quality icons. The left icon will tell Bridge to use any previews that are built into your documents to quickly display thumbnail images, while clicking on the right icon will produce a pop-up menu that allows you to choose between four choices:

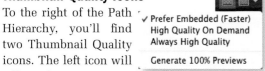

Prefer Embedded: This choice produces the same results as clicking on the left icon. It will use any embedded previews that are available to make thumbnail display as fast as possible (but it might not give you the highest quality preview).

High Quality On Demand: This is my favorite setting. It will use any embedded previews that are available and will render a higher quality preview once the image has been selected within Bridge.

Always High Quality: This choice will cause Bridge to open each individual image and produce a high quality thumbnail. This can take a considerable amount of time and is therefore not always the most practical setting to use when initially sorting a folder of images.

Generate 100% Previews: This option will cause Bridge to open each image and create a full resolution preview image. These large preview images take up a lot of space on your hard drive, which can limit their usefulness.

Filter Icon

Working our way toward the right, the next icon you'll find is the Filter icon. It allows you to only view images that have a particular star rating applied. You will find similar settings in the **Filter** panel that's usually found near the lower left of the Bridge window.

Sorting Pop-up Menu

You can change the order in which your images are displayed by choosing from the **Sort** pop-up menu. Clicking the triangle next to this pop-up menu will reverse the sort order.

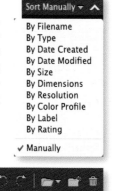

Other Icons

The rest of the icons that are found on the right side of the Path Bar are as follows: **Rotate Left**, **Rotate Right**, **Open Recent File**, **New Folder** and **Delete**. Most of these icons where available in previous versions of Bridge.

The **Open Recent File** choice might seem to be a repeat of the functionality that was found in a similar pop-up menu that's located near the upper left of the Bridge CS3 window, but there is an important difference: The CS3 pop-up menu only navigates to the *folder* that contains a file, while the CS4 **Open Recent File** pop-up menu actually opens the *file* without changing which folder you're browsing in Bridge.

Collections Panel

The new **Collections** panel (which replaces the Save as Collection button in the Find feature of Bridge CS3) is usually found near the lower left of the Bridge window. If it's not currently visible, choose **Collections** panel from the **Window** menu.

A Collection is in essence a virtual folder into which you can drag documents without actually changing the location of the documents on your hard drive. There are two types of Collections, Arbitrary and Smart Collections.

The Collections panel.

Arbitrary Collections

An Arbitrary collection (also known simply as a Collection) is one where the content is determined only by the documents you drag onto the collection (nothing is added automatically).

To create a collection just click on the **New Collection** icon that's found at the bottom of the **Collections** panel and drag any documents you desire onto the newly created collection.

Icons from left to right: Edit Smart Collection, New Collection, New Smart Collection, Delete Collection.

These documents can be located in multiple folders and can even be stored on multiple hard drives. When you click on the name of the collection, Bridge will display all the documents you've dragged onto the collection. To remove a document from a collection, select the document and then click the **Remove From Collection** button that's found above the thumbnail images.

I often use collections when setting up a slide show or getting ready for a speaking event. I simply drag the images I need to a collection and have instant access to what I need. It would also be very helpful putting together image presentations for clients.

Smart Collections

A Smart Collection is a collection that contains content that is automatically generated based on criteria you specify. To create a Smart Collection click the **New Smart Collection** icon at the bottom of the **Collections** panel.

In the dialog box that appears, the **Source** pop-up menu determines where Bridge will search for images and the Criteria area determines which images will be displayed. You can click the plus icon in the Criteria area to add additional search criteria. The **Match** pop-up menu will determine if a document must match all the criteria you've specified or if it would qualify by matching any of the criteria. The **Include Non-indexed Files** checkbox will cause Bridge to inspect all the images in the source folder even if Bridge has never inspected them before. That means that Bridge will have to spend time to read all the metadata for the images in the folder and it might take some time for you to see any results.

The concept of collections takes Bridge beyond the limitations of a simple file browser and allows you to more effectively organize your images.

You can create a Smart Collection based on the criteria shown above.

When you create a Smart Collection, you will be presented with this dialog box of options.

Output Panel

The Adobe **Out-put** panel (accessed either via the Output workspace or by choosing

Output to Web or PDF from the **Output** pop-up menu near the upper left of the Bridge window) replaces the old Web Photo Gallery, PDF Presentation and Contact Sheet II features from Bridge CS3. If the **Output** panel seems to be hiding, make sure all the panels in the Bridge window are expanded, which you do by dragging the divider bars that separate one panel from another.

PDF Photo Gallery

Clicking the **PDF** icon in the **Output** panel will present you with a vast array of options for creating PDF presentations.

At the top of the **Output** panel you'll find the **Template** pop-up menu where you can choose from predefined templates that change the Layout and Overlays settings in the panels below. Just below the **Template** pop-up menu, you'll find the **Refresh Preview** button, which will produce a preview in the **Output Preview** panel to the left of the settings you've specified. You're free to change the settings to modify the look of the preview and customize the presentation to your needs. There is a good number of options available; let's look at each section of settings one at a time.

| ✓ 2-UP Greeting Card |
| 2*2 Cells |
| 4 Wide |
| 4*5 Contact Sheet |
| 5*8 Contact Sheet |
| Fine Art Mat |
| Maximize Size |
| Triptych |

Document

The settings found under the Document heading determine the page size, background color and quality of your presentation. The Pass-

word settings allow you to prevent unauthorized viewing by assigning a password which would be required for opening, editing and/or printing the resulting PDF file.

Layout

The Layout section is where you can specify the top, bottom, left and right page margins, how many rows and columns of images you'd like

to use and how much space there should be between those rows and columns. The **Repeat One Photo per Page** option will allow you to create a separate page for each photo, in effect producing a picture package (such as six 2x3" photos on each page, depending on your layout settings).

Overlays

In this section, you can choose which if any text should appear along with the images and

style to be used for those elements. This is useful when you want a client to respond with the name of an image instead of a more generic description like "the one with the blue background."

Playback

The options in this section allow you to control what happens when the resulting document is first

opened. By turning on the **Advance Every** setting, you will in effect create an auto running slide show. There are many transition effects available, but I prefer to stick with the simplest choices so that the images used in the show are not overpowered by overly flashy transition effects.

Watermark

The **Watermark** settings will allow you to ghost some text over or under your images. The **Foreground** setting will place the over-laid text on top of the images,  while the **Background** setting will places the images on top of the text.

Once you have all the settings you want to use and you've previewed your presentation, you can click the **Save** button near the bottom of your screen to save the final PDF file.

Web Gallery

Clicking on the **Web Gallery** icon at the top of the **Output** panel will present you with a panel full of op-  tions you can use to create and customize a web photo gallery. Much of this functionality used to be available through Bridge CS3 and involved an Automate feature which opened up Photoshop to create the web gallery. Now this feature is completely owned and operated by Bridge which means you can create web galleries to your heart's content while Photoshop is busy doing other things. In addition to its new residence, this feature took on a few bells and whistles that are truly helpful, such as the ability to upload your gallery to a web server directly from the **Web Gallery Output** panel.

At the top of the panel, a **Template** pop-up menu allows you to start from a preexisting example. Some of the templates offer multiple color or thumbnail size choices which can be chosen from the **Style** pop-up menu. Once you've deter- mined the template you'd like to use, click the **Refresh Preview** button to see how the images (that you've selected in Bridge) would look using that template. From there you've got multiple options for your gallery, which we'll look at top to bottom.

Site Info

The settings in the Site Info section will de- termine the text that will appear on your web gal- lery. The gallery title will display in the upper left, the **Gallery Caption** in the upper right and the **Your Name** setting will ap- pear below the **Gallery Caption**.  Any text you enter in the **About This Gallery** field will be made available to your viewer when they choose **About This Gallery** from the pop-up menu that appears after clicking on the **View** option (which is below the gallery name in your web gallery). Clicking on the **Your Name** information in the web gallery will allow your viewer to cre- ate a new e-mail that uses the name and e-mail address settings you entered in the **E-mail Ad- dress** field.

Color Palette

The settings in the Color Palette section deter- mine the color that will be used for various ele- ments in your web gallery. The 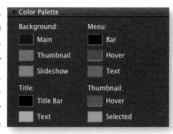 appearance of the palette will shift to correspond to the Template selected. See the example shown here to get an idea of where each color is used.

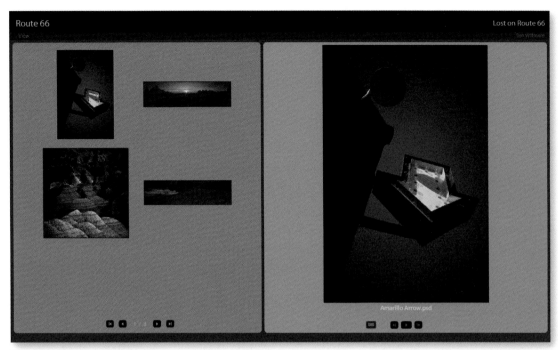

The image above is an example of a Web Photo Gallery created using the settings shown in screen shots on the previous page. I made it look this ugly so you'd have a good idea of what each one of the color choices would affect.

Appearance

Turning on the **Show File Names** checkbox will cause the file name of each image to be displayed below the  image when it is previewed in the web gallery. In this section you can also set the size of the thumbnail image and how large of a preview will be displayed when you click on a thumbnail.

Create Gallery

Once you've finalized the look of your site, you should enter a name for the Gallery to determine the text that will appear in the web browser's title bar. Then you can decide if you'd like to save the web site  to your hard drive or upload it directly to your web server. If you plan to upload the site directly, you'll need to know all the information that is necessary to log into your web server. If you don't know this information, contact the company that hosts your web site and ask them for the settings shown at the bottom of the **Output** panel.

Preferences

Choosing **Preferences** from the **Adobe Bridge CS4** menu (Mac), or **Edit** menu (Win) and choosing the Output section will present you with a few choices that are specific to the **Output** panel.

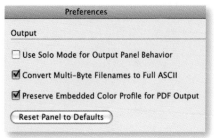 *The Output section of the Bridge Preferences dialog box.*

Solo Mode: This option is useful when working on a small monitor such as those found on most laptops. It will only allow one section of the **Output** panel to be viewed at a time. Clicking on the title of any section will expand it while collapsing all others.

Convert Multi-Byte Filenames to Full ASCII: Turn this option on if you find that your web browser or FTP service is having trouble displaying or uploading images that contain non-ASCII characters (files names that contain unusual symbols or foreign language characters for example). This will cause all those non-standard characters to be converted into a format that just about any web browser or FTP service can understand.

Preserve Embedded Color Profile for PDF Output: This checkbox will make sure that all the images used in a PDF presentation have the information needed to be displayed accurately. I'd suggest you leave this checkbox turned on at all times, unless you have a specialized use that does not require it.

Reset Panel to Defaults: This button will clear out all the text that you've entered in various fields within the **Output** panel and set all the colors back to their defaults.

Output Module Script

If you find that you won't be using the **Output** panel and would rather have Bridge load faster and take up less memory by preventing it from loading the **Output** panel altogether, feel free to turn off the appropriate checkbox in the Startup Scripts section of the **Preferences** dialog box.

✓ **Adobe Output Module**
  Enables the Output Panel for PDF creation and web galleries.

Misc. Changes

Now that we've finished exploring the more obvious changes made in Bridge, let's dig deeper and look at the settings you might not notice at first glance.

View Options

The **View** menu has a few new options in Bridge CS4 including:

Full Screen Preview: Choosing this option will cause the image you have selected to be scaled to fit your screen. You can toggle this view by pressing the **Spacebar**. If you have multiple images selected they will display in slide show fashion, one image at a time, and you can use your arrow keys to more back and forth within the selected images.

Show Items from Subfolders: This replaces an icon that used to be found in the **Filter** panel back in the CS3 version of Bridge. When this option is turned on, Bridge will display all the items in the current folder and any subfolders that are contained within the folder you are viewing.

Review Mode: We already talked about this mode earlier in this chapter, but we accessed it via the **Refine** pop-up menu instead of the **View** menu. You simply have two methods for getting to the same mode.

Preferences

We've already talked about a few of the new Preferences in Bridge CS4. Now let's take a look at the settings we haven't had a chance to cover.

General Preferences: They've added a new setting that allows you to **Command-click** (Mac), or **Ctrl-click** (Win) on an image when viewing it as a preview or while in Review mode. If this option is turned off, then simply clicking (without command/control held) will display the loupe. That's a nice option to have if you find that you often accidently click on your images and are annoyed at the loupe appearing when you don't want it.

☐ ⌘+Click Opens the Loupe When Previewing or Reviewing

Thumbnails Preferences: Adobe increased the **Do Not Process File Larger Than** setting from the old setting of **400Mb** all the way up to **1000MB**. That makes sense now that the resolution of digital cameras is being pushed higher and higher each year. Complex layered files produced from these high resolution cameras can easily approach 1GB in size.

Performance and File Handling

Do Not Process Files Larger Than: 1000 MB

Previously cached files will not be affected by changes to this setting. This setting takes effect after the cache has been purged.

Cache Preferences: They've added a new **Keep 100% Previews in Cache** setting, which will cause Bridge to maintain any 100% previews it has generated. Be careful using this setting because some of those previews can be extremely large and will quickly fill up your hard drive. They also changed the **Cache Size** setting to make it easier to tell how many images sill be stored in the cache. In CS3 they just used generic terms like Large and Small.

Cache Size: 10,000 ———△——— 500,000

Sets the maximum number of items stored in the cache. A higher number improves performance but consumes more disk space.

Advanced Preferences: They added a new **Generate Monitor-Size Previews** setting which causes Bridge to generate previews that are the same size as the largest monitor you have attached to your computer, instead of the standard 1024x1024 pixel preview size. This can be useful when working with a large display (such as a 30-inch) because the smaller 1024 pixel previews can appear to be of low quality on such a large display. They also added a **Start Bridge At Login** preference which will cause Bridge to launch when you boot your computer so you won't have to wait for it to launch when you want to start browsing files.

☐ Generate Monitor-Size Previews

Generates previews based on the resolution of the largest monitor. Purge cache to regenerate existing previews.

☐ Start Bridge At Login

During system login launch Bridge in the background so that it is instantly available when needed.

Stacks

Stacks are not new to this version of Bridge, but Adobe did add a few convenience features in CS4. Before we get into what's new, let's take a quick look at how Stacks work.

To create a stack, select multiple images in Bridge and choose **Group as Stack** from the **Stacks** menu You can also type **Command-G** (Mac), or **Ctrl-G** (Win). That will cause the images to appear as a literal stack of thumbnail images with a number in the upper left corner that indicates how many images are contained in the stack. You can click the number to expand the stack and view all the images contained within it and then click the number a second time to collapse the stack once again.

A collapsed stack.

An expanded stack containing three images.

Clicking on the top image of a collapsed stack will select only the top image in the stack. If you want to select the entire stack, click within the edge of the underlying images (just to the right of the edge of the top image).

Left: The top image in the stack is selected. Right: The entire stack is selected.

To remove an image from a stack, select one or more stacked images and drag it next to one of the documents that are not part of the stack, or choose **Ungroup from Stack** from the **Stacks** menu.

Now that you have a general idea of how they work, let's explore the changes Adobe made to stacks in Photoshop CS4.

Auto-Stack Panorama/HDR

Choosing **Auto-Stack Panorama/HDR** from the **Stacks** menu will cause Bridge to analyze the documents in the folder you're currently browsing and group series of panorama or bracketed exposures into stacks. Bridge will analyze the metadata from the documents to determine what should be considered a panorama or HDR bracket. If the exposure is relatively consistent and the time between shots is very brief, Bridge will consider the series of document to be a panorama. If the exposure setting varies but the time between shots is still very brief Bridge will consider a series of documents to be an HDR bracket.

> **NOTE**
>
> **High Dynamic Range**
> HDR is an acronym for High Dynamic Range. An HDR image is one that was created by merging multiple exposures that vary in brightness in an attempt to capture the full brightness range of a scene that is beyond the six stop range that most digital cameras can capture.

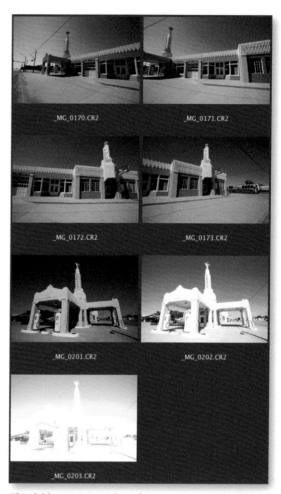

This folder contains a four shot panorama and a three exposure HDR bracket.

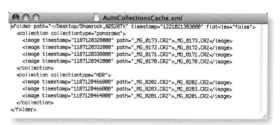

The Auto-Stack Panorama/HDR command produces a text file that is used by the Process Collections in Photoshop command to determine which files should be combined into a panorama or HDR image.

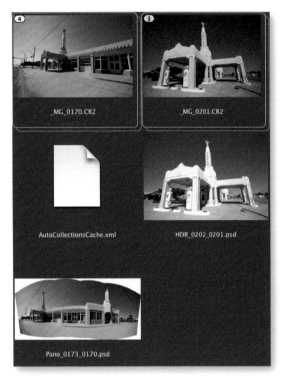

After choosing Auto-Stack Panorama/HDR, the images were grouped into two stacks and an .xml file was created.

A small text file that has a file extension of .xml will be created in the same folder as the stacks to indicate which series of images was considered a panorama and which were considered an HDR bracket.

Process Collections in Photoshop

Once you've applied the **Auto-Stack Panorama/HDR** command to a folder, you can go to Photoshop and choose **Tools>Photoshop>Process Collections** to have Photoshop read the .xml file and apply **Photomerge** to the panoramas and **Merge to HDR** to the HDR brackets.

If no .xml file is found in the folder you are browsing, the **Process Collections in Photoshop** command will create its own .xml file in the same way that the **Auto-Stack Panorama/HDR** command would, but it will not group each series into a stack.

These new features make it easy to have Photoshop run unattended and process images that would usually require quite a bit of user interaction and patience.

If you don't plan to use the auto-stack feature, you can disable the features by turning off the **Auto Collection CS4** in the **Startup Scripts** area of Bridge's **Preferences** dialog box.

Choosing Process Collections in Photoshop caused two new files to be created.

Scrub Through Large Stacks

When a stack contains more than ten images, a play button and scrubber bar will appear near the top of the collapsed stack. Clicking the play button will quickly cycle through the images to produce a movie effect. Dragging the black circle across the scrubber bar will also cycle through the images based on how quickly you drag your mouse.

A scrubber bar and play button will appear at the top edge of stacks that contain more than ten images.

Load Files Into Layers

You'll find the new **Load Files into Layers** command under the **Tools>Photoshop** menu. It will open any selected images and copy their contents into a single document as separate layers. This is something you could do in Bridge CS3 if you had downloaded the Dr. Brown's Services scripts from www.RussellBrown.com.

Gesture Support

If you own one of the newest Mac laptops you'll be able to use multi-finger gestures to navigate through slide shows in Bridge. Here's a sample of what's possible:

Three Finger Swipe: Swipe three fingers across your trackpad horizontally to advance to the previous or next image.

Spread to Zoom: Place two fingers together on the trackpad and then separate them to zoom into your image.

Pinch to Zoom Out: Place two fingers apart on the trackpad and pinch them together to zoom out on your image.

Drag up/down to zoom: You can also place two fingers together on the trackpad and drag up or down to zoom in or out on your image.

Tiny Changes

Some of these changes are not all that obvious if you're casually browsing around Bridge's interface. To some they might seem insignificant but to others they could have a big impact on their work in Photoshop.

Faster Performance: Bridge can now handle folders that contain tens of thousands of images. Older versions would choke on such a task.

3D File Format Previews: 3D files that can be opened in the Extended version of Photoshop can now be previewed within Bridge.

Manage Extensions: There is a new feature found under the **Help** menu for managing Bridge extensions.

Enough time has passed since the introduction of Bridge (remember when it was called the File Browser?) that we now take all this file management wizardry for granted. Much of what we can now do in Bridge in just a few minutes used to take hours, and for photographers in particular, who struggle with organizing and managing thousands upon thousands of images, Bridge is a lifesaver.

What does this all mean? It means that any of you folks who are still sitting on hard drives full of old, moldy folders containing badly organized, poorly identified images no longer have any kind of reasonable excuse to put off cleaning house.

Don't let all of these marvelous features go to waste. If you've been meaning to get your images sorted and prepared for cataloging so you can sell stock photos, the new **Collections** panel and enhanced **File Info** dialog box will be an invaluable aid. If you've been putting off creating web galleries so you can showcase your work, the new **Output** panel and web gallery templates will make it a snap. Or, if it's just family photos you've been neglecting because they're hopelessly disorganized in haphazardly named folders strewn all over your hard drive (the last Christmas photo you printed was when...?), now is the time to let Bridge help you work through it all. So, what are you waiting for? Go clean your room!

Chapter 2
Camera Raw 5.0

ACTING MORE LIKE A SOVEREIGN NATION and less like a plug-in appendage, Camera Raw 5.0 has strayed even farther from the mothership by adding features that make it less essential than ever to venture into Photoshop. You can now adjust isolated areas of an image, apply vignetting after cropping, and much more.

Below is an overview of the new Adobe Camera Raw (ACR) features we'll be covering in this chapter:

- **Adjustment Brush:** This new brush allows you to apply adjustments to isolated areas of an image, which not only makes ACR much more versatile, but makes you less dependent on Photoshop for your adjustments.
- **Graduated Filter:** Simulates a traditional graduated neutral density filter (commonly used to resuscitate landscape images with flat, washed out skies) by allowing you to apply adjustments that fade out slowly as they pass over an area.
- **Post Crop Vignetting:** This new feature, which boasts four levels of control, allows you to quickly lighten or darken the edges of your images, even after cropping them.
- **Miscellaneous Improvements:** In addition to the stars of the ACR upgrade, there are some less conspicuous gems waiting to be discovered, including Crop Preview, expanded JPEG and TIFF capability, compatibility with Lightroom 2.0, and a new profile editor.

Where's My Stuff?

Surprisingly, Adobe hasn't done all that much to mess with your mind in the 5.0 version of ACR. Instead of deleting or changing features, they've mostly added to what's already there. However, just to keep you on your toes, here is one thing to keep in mind as you navigate the new territory:

- **Preference Camera Raw:** Bridge used to feature a preference for how to handle opening JPEG and TIFF with Adobe Camera Raw. Those settings have been replaced with similar ones in the Camera Raw **Preferences** dialog box which can be accessed under the **Adobe Bridge CS4** menu (Mac), or **Edit** menu (Win).

Adjustment Brush

The new Adjustment Brush in Adobe Camera Raw 5.0 (ACR) allows you to make adjustments to isolated areas within an image. This new capability makes ACR a much more powerful adjustment tool, allowing many images to be adjusted from start-to-finish in a single dialog box instead of having to rely on the sophisticated clutter of windows, bars, and panels that make up the Photoshop interface.

NOTE

Accessing Camera Raw
*To access the Adobe Camera Raw dialog box (also known as ACR), choose a non-layered TIFF, JPEG or RAW format image in Bridge and choose **File>Open in Camera Raw**.*

After clicking on the new **Adjustment Brush** icon at the top of the ACR window, you can move your mouse over  your image and paint to brighten the image. The default settings will cause the area over which you paint to have its **Exposure** setting increased by +0.50. You can change this behavior before or after painting by adjusting the sliders found on the right side the ACR window.

Brush Settings

You can control how your brush interacts with the image by adjusting the brush settings that are found below the adjustment sliders located on the right side of the ACR window. Here's an overview of the settings:

Size: Controls the diameter of your brush as indicated by the brush cursor shown below. In addition to dragging the slider, you can change this setting by pressing the] and [keys on your keyboard (which is also how you control your brush size in Photoshop).

Feather: This setting determines the quality (hard or soft) of the edge of the Adjustment Brush. You can see just how soft the brush is by the way it appears when you mouse over your image. The inner circle indicates the edge of the solid portion of your brush, while the dashed circle shows you the halfway point of the fade out. The farther the dashed circle is from the solid one, the softer the edge of the brush.

Flow: The **Flow** setting determines the percentage of the adjustment that will be applied on your first pass over the image. Using a setting below 100% allows you to paint over an area in multiple passes to build up the effect.

Density: This setting allows you to limit the total amount of adjustment that can be applied when painting over the image.

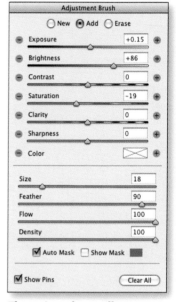

The settings above will appear on the right side of the Camera Raw window when the Adjustment Brush is active. The sliders at the top control the adjustment that will be applied, while the sliders at the bottom determine the type of brush will be used to isolate an area.

Density works in concert with the **Flow** setting. **Density** is the maximum amount of adjustment you'll apply regardless of how many times your brush strokes overlap. **Density** works much like the **Opacity** setting for brushes in Photoshop. **Flow**, on the other hand, is the percentage of **Density** you'd like to apply with each stroke.

Painting over your image while both the **Flow** and **Density** settings are at 100% will apply the full force of the adjustment in a single stroke. Lowering the **Flow** setting to 20% while keeping **Density** at 100% will apply 20% of the adjustment in the first stroke. Overlapping your strokes will cause the adjustment to build up. If you paint across an area enough times using these settings, you'll eventually reach the full amount of the **Density** setting (100% in this case). Lowering the **Density** setting to 50% while keeping the **Flow** setting at 20% makes things a little bit more complicated. In this case, your first brush stroke will cause 10% of the adjustment to apply because you're getting 20% of the 50% Density setting (20% of 50%=10%). Subsequent strokes will build up the effect, but will never get above 50%, as determined by the **Density** setting.

New, Add & Erase: The **New**, **Add** and **Erase** settings that appear above the adjustment sliders determine how your next brush stroke will affect the image. When you click the Adjustment Brush the first time, this setting is automatically set to **New**, and will behave as I've described above. You'll notice that when you brush over your image, as soon as you release your mouse button, the setting automatically switches to **Add**. When it's set to **Add**, subsequent painting will increase the amount of adjustment being applied. Using the **Erase** setting will cause subsequent strokes to reduce the amount of adjustment being applied. Your brush settings will change when you switch between these two modes, allowing you to erase with a hard-edged brush while adding with a soft brush.

You can hold the **Option** key (Mac), or **Alt** key (Win) to temporarily toggle between the **Add** and **Erase** settings. The only problem with using the keyboard commands above is that you cannot use keyboard shortcuts to change the **Size** or **Feature** settings, which makes this option a lot less useful than it could have been.

Auto Mask: When this setting is turned off, adjustments are applied based on a combination of the **Size**, **Feather**, **Flow** and **Density** settings in use. Turning on the **Auto Mask** setting (via the checkbox, or by typing **M**) will cause Camera Raw to pay attention to the tiny crosshair that appears in the center of your brush. As you paint across the image, the stroke will be limited to affecting areas that are similar in brightness, color and texture to the areas the crosshair passes over. That can be a great help when you want to isolate the subject of a photograph from its background, but only when there is a noticeable difference between your background and subject, and the background is relatively simple.

Don't rely on one method for masking your image. You might find it useful to start with the **Auto Mask** feature turned on to isolate a general area, but then you might run into difficulties when attempting to remove areas with **Auto Mask** turned on. When that's the case, just turn off the **Auto Mask** checkbox, set the brush to **Erase**, and manually remove areas from the mask by painting.

Top left: Original, unadjusted image.

Top right: Result of using the Adjustment Brush with Auto Masking turned on.

Lower left: Mask overlay that shows result of painting while the Auto Mask feature is active.

Show Mask: It can be difficult to tell which areas of an image you've changed after painting with the Adjustment Brush. Turning on the **Show Mask** checkbox will cause the brush strokes that you've applied to appear as a colored overlay. This is a nice way to see if you've accurately isolated an area, or if you have a bunch of overspray in places you didn't want to adjust. You are free to paint while this overlay is visible, and you can toggle the mask by typing **Y** on your keyboard.

If the color of the mask is too similar to the color of your image, it will be difficult to see its edges, making it less precise. To change the color of the overlay, click on the color swatch to the right of the **Show Mask** checkbox. That will produce a color picker where you can select the color, brightness, and opacity of the color. There is also a **Color Indicate** option, which dictates whether the color will indicate areas you've painted on (affected areas), or areas you've left alone (unaffected areas).

Now that you have an idea of how Camera Raw's masking feature works, we'll move on, but first take a look at an example of how you might use all those features to isolate an area. In the images to the right, I wanted to mask an adjustment so that it would only affect the chrome and black Route 66 sculpture.

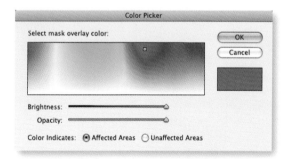

Clicking on the color swatch to the right of the Show Mask checkbox will produce this color picker.

The is the original image as it appeared in Camera Raw before any masking had been applied.

Result of using the Auto Mask feature to create a mask.

Result of removing lower overspray using Auto Mask.

Changing the color of the mask made it easier to see that there was overspray on the sky near the upper left of the sculpture.

Attempting to remove the overspray while Auto Mask was active was not successful, so I turned off Auto Mask and manually removed the overspray. At this point I turned off the Show Mask checkbox and used the adjustment sliders to change the look of the image.

Adjustment Settings

You can change the brush's adjustment sliders found on the right side of the **Camera Raw** dialog box at any time. Changing them before you paint on your image can feel a little odd since you won't see any preview of the changes within your image (you'd have to paint to determine which areas should change). Moving the sliders after painting will interactively change the look of your image and the adjustment will be limited to the area you isolated with your brush strokes. You can continue to paint at any time in the process to increase or decrease the area that is affected.

You can also toggle the **Preview** checkbox that appears above the image to see what your image looked like before and after the changes you've made with the Adjustment Brush.

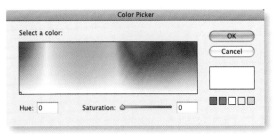

Click on the color swatch associated with the Color adjustment to access this color picker.

The New Color Adjustment

Most of the adjustment sliders are copies of what are found in the main adjustment area of the **Camera Raw** window. The only exception is the new Color adjustment which allows you to shift the color of your image toward the color you choose from a color picker.

To access the color picker, click on the color swatch that appears opposite the word Color near the right edge of the adjustment sliders. The five swatches that appear in the lower right of the color picker are simply presets that allow you to quickly make your image warmer or cooler (these same presets can be accessed by clicking the **Plus** and **Minus** icons to the left and right of the Color adjustment area). Clicking the middle swatch will reset the dialog box, effectively cancelling the color adjustment. Click and drag within the large color field to choose the general color you'd like to use and then adjust the **Saturation** slider to control the strength of the adjustment.

Result of using a Color adjustment to shift the image toward blue.

Original, unadjusted image.

Result of using a Color adjustment to shift the image toward yellow.

Working with Pins

When you modify an image using the **Adjustment Brush**, the area you isolate will be marked with a **Pin** icon on top of your image.

You can add additional pins by choosing the **New** option that appears above the adjustment sliders and then clicking within your image to begin masking an area. The green pin with a black dot in the center indicates the adjustment you are currently editing. Any pins that appear gray indicate previous adjustments that are not currently being edited. You can click any pin to make it active and then make further changes to the mask or adjustment sliders to update the pin.

Each of the four pins represents an isolated area where I've performed an adjustment using the Adjustment Brush.

You can also move your mouse over a pin to temporarily view the mask associated with the pin. That makes it very easy to figure out which area each pin in affecting.

A quick way to adjust multiple areas is to use the **Plus** and **Minus** icons that appear to the left and right of each adjustment slider. Clicking one of those icons will automatically choose the **New** option, zero out all the sliders and then increase or decrease the setting for the slider you clicked next to. That way you're all set to click and drag within your image and add a new pin. Moving back and forth between those icons and the image makes complex changes very easy. Just click and drag within your image to isolate an area, move the sliders to fine-tune the adjustment, and click the **Plus** or **Minus** icons next to another slider to get ready to adjust another isolated area.

Clicking the **Clear All** button that's found below the adjustment sliders will delete all the pins from your image returning it to how it appeared before you ever used the **Adjustment Brush**. To delete a single pin, click on the pin you wish to remove and press the **Delete** key.

The four images above show what you would see if you hovered over each of the four pins that were used to adjust this image.

This is the original, un-adjusted image as it looked before the Adjustment Brush was used to enhance the image.

This is the result of using the Adjustment Brush on four areas of the image. One to darken the sky, one to lighten the rocks, one to add contrast to the water and one to shift the color of my skin.

Graduated Filter

A traditional graduated neutral density filter is used by photographers to adjust how much light from bright portions of a scene reaches the camera's film or sensor. It is especially helpful in improving scenes that have flat, washed out skies. ACR 5.0 has attempted to simulate the effect with its new **Graduated Filter**, which can be found in the icon bar at the top of the Camera Raw window. Clicking on the icon and dragging across your image will create an adjustment that fades out in the direction in which you dragged.

The green and red marking in the image above indicates where the Graduated Filter has been applied.

The point at which you first click determines where the adjustment will be applied at full strength (as marked by a green circle), and the point where you release the mouse button determines where the adjustment will stop fading out (as marked by a red circle). The angle at which you drag is important because it determines the angle of the fade out (as indicated by the dashed line that connects the red and green circles). Dashed red and green lines also mark where the adjustment will start to apply at full strength and where it will stop fading out. Any area that appears beyond the dashed green line will also get the full strength of the adjustment. Holding **Shift** while dragging will constrain the angle of the **Graduated Filter** to an increment of 15° (0°, 15°, 30°, 45°, etc.), which can make it easier to make a perfectly vertical or horizontal line.

The same adjustment sliders that were available with the Adjustment Brush are also available in the Graduated Filter. You can change the adjustment sliders at any time before or after you've dragged across your image to apply an adjustment. You can create multiple adjustments by choosing the **New** choice that's available above the adjustment sliders (or typing **N**) and dragging across the image once again. The adjustment you are actively editing will appear in color, while all the other adjustments will appear as two white circles.

Left: Active adjustment.
Right: Non-active adjustment.

Original image where the bottom left corner is too dark.

Result of applying the Graduated Filter to the lower left portion of the image.

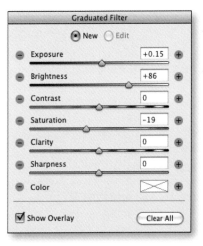
The adjustment settings used to adjust the image above.

Post Crop Vignetting

The concept of vignetting is not new to this version of Camera Raw (it's been available under the Lens Corrections tab). Traditionally, vignetting is the effect you get when the light going through your camera lens falls off as it reaches the corners of the frame. This produces dark corners that could be compensated for with ACR's **Lens Vignetting** setting.

Many people use this effect to purposefully darken the edges of their images in an attempt to draw the viewer's attention to the subject of the photograph. This was fine as long as you did not crop the image. Past versions of the **Lens Vignetting** feature always applied to the edge of the uncropped image and once cropped, the vignetting effect would be lost.

ACR 5.0 has fixed that problem with a new **Post Crop Vignetting** feature that is much more useful when you want to darken the edges of an image you plan on cropping. It darkens the edges of an image based on its cropped size instead of starting from the original uncropped image. (Actually, you could also lighten the edges of an image using this feature, but most folks go for the darkening effect.)

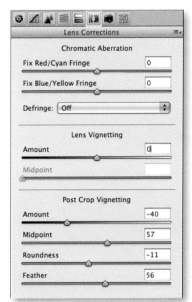
The Vignetting settings are found under the Lens Corrections tab in ACR.

The following settings are available when applying **Post Crop Vignetting**:

Amount: Determines how much brightening (positive numbers), or darkening (negative numbers) will be applied to the vignetting area.

Amount -30   *Amount -80*

Midpoint: Determines where the halfway point of the fade out will appear. Low numbers bring it closer to the center of the image, while high numbers push it toward the edge of the image.

Midpoint 80   *Midpoint 20*

Roundness: Determines the shape created by the vignetting. When this setting is at zero, the shape of the vignette will have the same proportions as the image to which it's being applied. Using positive numbers will make the shape closer to a circle whereas negative settings produce more of a rectangle with rounded corners look.

Roundness +80   *Roundness -80*

Feather: This setting determines how quickly the darkening effect will fade out as it approaches the center of the image. Lower settings produce crisper edges, while high settings produce softer edges.

Feather 80   *Feather 20*

Left: Image before cropping has been applied.
Right: A cropped version of the image before vignetting.

Result of applying Lens Vignetting.

Result of applying Post Crop Vignetting.

Misc. Improvements

We've looked at all the big, headline-grabbing features in ACR 5.0, now let's give some of the little guys a turn. For some of you, these smaller changes might be a big deal. They are:

Crop Preview: In previous versions, cropping an image would produce a cropping rectangle, but you were not able to see the end result without opening the image in Photoshop. In ACR 5.0, switching from the **Crop** tool to any other tool will finish the crop and present you with a cropped preview image.

Left: Previous versions always showed the full frame. Right: Result in the new version.

JPEG and TIFF Preferences: Adobe has given us more control over how Camera Raw will handle opening JPEG and TIFF files. In Adobe **Bridge CS4>Camera Raw Preferences**, the three new choices allow you to: **1)** Prevent all TIFF and JPEGs from being opened into ACR, **2)** Only open those files that have been adjusted with ACR and have raw settings attached to them, **3)** Open all JPEG and TIFF files that Camera Raw can handle.

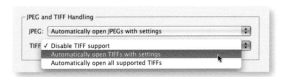

Better Auto Results: They've improved the results you get when clicking **Auto** button in the **Basic** tab of Camera Raw. The adjustment is now less likely to produce blown out highlights.

Camera Raw Icon in Bridge: You'll find a new **Open in Camera Raw** icon near the top of the Bridge window that allows you to open compatible files with a single click. If a file you've selected is not compatible, this icon will simply be grayed out.

Spot Removal Opacity: If you'd rather tone down a defect instead of removing it completely, you'll like the results you get from cloning or healing with the new **Opacity** setting in the **Spot Removal** tool (found in the icon bar at the top of the Camera Raw window).

From left to right: Original image, retouched with opacity of 50%, retouched at 100% opacity.

Negative Clarity: The **Clarity** slider (found in both the **Basic** tab of Camera Raw, as well in as the new **Adjustment Brush** settings) can now be moved in a negative direction. It will produce a softening effect which opens up all sorts of possibilities, especially when used selectively with the **Adjustment Brush**. It's great for things like reducing the impact of pores on skin and shiny spots on faces, or producing an artistic, soft-focus effect.

Top left: Clarity zero
Top right: Clarity -40
Bottom: Clarity +40

Compatibility with Lightroom 2.0: Camera Raw can now handle files that have been processed using Adobe Lightroom 2.0. You just have to make sure that Lightroom is set up to save adjustments in sidecar XMP files or use DNG files which don't require a sidecar XMP file (just as with previous versions).

Backwards Compatibility: This is more of a warning than a feature. Be careful when giving images to others that have been processed in ACR 5.0. If they are using an older version of ACR and you give them a file that utilizes some of the new features in ACR 5.0, those changes will be ignored. To prevent this from happening, open the image into Photoshop and save it as a JPEG or TIFF file. Opening the image makes the changes permanent, so the newly saved version will contain all the changes you've made in the new version.

Profile Editor: If you don't like the look of your images with default settings in ACR, or would like to profile your camera for more precise results, you can now download a camera profile editor from the following web site: **http://labs.adobe.com/wiki/index.php/DNG_Profiles.** This new utility is designed for advanced users who love to tweak every setting to get the best results. It also has an area that allows you to profile your camera using a Macbeth Colorchecker. That would be useful for many studio shooters.

As you can see, Adobe Camera Raw continues to evolve with Photoshop CS4. I find the **Post Crop Vignetting** and new **Adjustment Brush** to be my two favorite new features. I just wish Adobe wouldn't insist on offering ACR as an import plug-in to Photoshop. I think it would be much more versatile if it was offered as an Adjustment Layer in the main area of Photoshop.

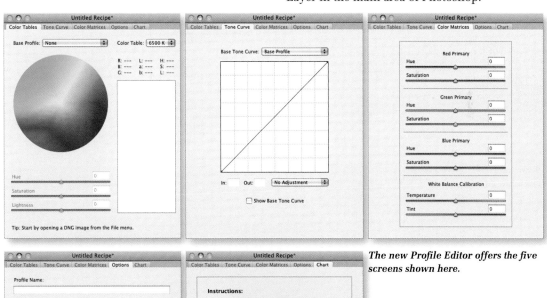

The new Profile Editor offers the five screens shown here.

Chapter 3
Interface Changes

I N THEIR QUEST TO "DRAMATICALLY REDEFINE" PHOTOSHOP, Adobe didn't hold back when it came to tampering with the interface. If you thought you could rest easy after the interface overhaul in CS3 (where palettes began morphing into panels), think again. This latest incarnation is more than a nip and tuck, and will surely inspire its share of both fans and critics.

Below is an overview of what we'll be covering in this chapter:

- **Terminology:** As Photoshop changes, so does some of the terminology, so we'll take a quick language course to get us all on the same page.
- **Redesigned Panels:** Learn about the revamped palettes—now and forever called *panels*—and how they can be more versatile and efficient than the previous design.
- **Application Bar:** This extra row of icons saves space on Windows but can waste it on a Mac without adding much new to the interface.
- **Tabbed Windows:** Just like tabbed web browsing, you can now view your documents in a tabbed arrangement. This new feature makes it much easier to switch between documents, and gives you a tidier workspace.
- **Application Frame:** Mac users can opt for a big gray box that houses the entire interface, making it easier to work on multiple monitors.
- **Misc. Changes:** Learn about the less noticeable changes they've made in how you interact with Photoshop as a whole, including a new capability that allows developers to create their own panels using Adobe Flash.

Where's My Stuff?

Some of features you're used to working with have been moved or redesigned. Here's what to look for in the new interface:

- **Palette, Who?:** The word, "palette" has been given the boot in favor of "panel," so things like "**Palette Options**" in the **Layers** panel side menu are now called "**Panel Options**."
- **Bridge Icon:** The Bridge icon that used to appear near the upper right of the Photoshop window has been redesigned and moved to the left side of the new Application bar near the top of your screen.
- **Screen Mode Icon:** If you're used to changing between screen modes using the **Screen Mode** icon that was found at the bottom of the Tool bar, you'll want to look for a similar icon in the new Application bar at the top of your screen.
- **Maximum Screen Mode:** This mode is no longer available and has not been replaced by anything. Why they added it in CS3 only to remove it now makes no sense to me.

- **Panels in Full Screen Mode:** In CS3, your panels would be visible after switching to **Full Screen** mode (by typing **F** twice or choosing it from the **Screen Mode** icon). To accomplish the same thing in CS4 you'll have to get used to pressing **Tab** to make them visible. The new default setting automatically hides the panels when entering **Full Screen** mode.

- **Panel Icons:** The icons used for closing and collapsing tabs and panels have been replaced with new behaviors. To collapse a panel, double-click on any of the tabs contained within it. To close a tab or the entire panel, click the appropriate choice from the side menu of the panel.

- **Default Workspace:** In CS3, you could reset all your panels and keyboard shortcuts to their default settings by choosing **Default Workspace** from the **Window>Workspace** menu. In Photoshop CS4, you have to choose **Essentials** from the same menu to get back to the defaults.

- **Dock of Panel Icons:** The default workspace in CS3 displayed a small vertical dock full of icons that made accessing many panels very convenient. By default, that dock is no longer visible and there is no workspace that automatically recreates it. If you liked working with it, you'll have to construct a replacement panel and then save it as a workspace so you can easily retrieve it when needed.

- **Workspace Menu:** If the **Window>Workspace** menu was a common stop for you in CS3, it might take a while for you to get used the new layout in CS4. They've moved the user-created presets to the top of the menu to make them easier to select, they've removed the choice to reset panel locations, menus and keyboard shortcuts, and they've removed or renamed many of the default workspaces.

- **Help Shortcuts:** The index of help topics that was found at the bottom of the **Help** menu has been removed. Photoshop's help system now uses your default web browser and features an index on the left side of its interface.

Terminology

Let's start with some terminology just to make sure we're on the same page when talking about Photoshop's revised interface. Here are the general terms you'll find me throwing around in this chapter:

It's a Panel, Not a Palette: Traditionally we've always called them palettes, those little floating boxes that house many of the features that help you monitor and modify your work in Photoshop. They contain things like Layers, Swatches and Channels and are listed under the **Window** menu at the top of your screen. In CS3, Adobe introduced the use of the word, "panel," which to everyone's confusion they used interchangeably with the word, "palette." In CS4, Adobe banished the word "palette" altogether and though I am fond of this little word (we've been together for over a decade), for the sake of continuity I am following suit. So, from now on, it's (gulp!) a *panel*. I'm sure a huge percentage of Photoshop users will continue to think of it as a palette, and if you are among the faithful, I don't blame you.

Tab: Each panel has a Tab at the top to identify it from the others. Clicking and dragging on a tab will move a single panel.

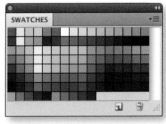

Tab Group: Tabs (and the panels they are attached to) can be stored together in a Tab Group. Just drag one tab onto another to group them together. To move all the tabs that are contained in a group, drag in the empty space to the right of the tabs.

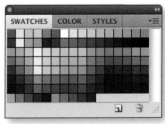

Bar: Photoshop's tools and main options are contained in bars. A bar is much like a panel, but they do not have tabs at the top and cannot be grouped together, and they can't be resized (very much). The three bars you'll find in Photoshop are the Tool bar on the left of your screen, Options bar and new Application bar, both of which are located at the top of your screen. When you press **Tab**, you'll toggle the visibility of all the panels and bars. Pressing **Shift-Tab** will toggle the visibility of the panels while leaving the bars visible.

Dock: Panels and Tab Groups can be stacked into what is often referred to as a dock. To stack one or more panels, drag the tab from one panel to the bottom edge of another panel. Docks can be snapped to the edge of your screen by dragging the dock's dark gray bar (that

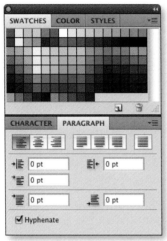

appears at its top) to the edge of your screen.

Minimize: Double-clicking on the tab at the top of any panel will minimize the panel (or the group it's contained within) so all you can see is its name. Double-click a second time to maximize the panel once again.

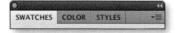

Collapse: Clicking the double arrow icon that appears in the upper right of Groups and Docks (anywhere on the dark gray bar really) will collapse them into icons. Once you've

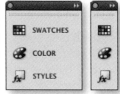

collapsed something into an icon, you can drag on its right edge to determine the amount of space that will be available for the identifying text.

Now that you have some idea of the terms I might throw at you, and you're in the know about a palette being a panel, let's start to explore some of the interface changes in CS4.

Redesigned Panels

Adobe has yet again changed the look of the panels that make up the Photoshop interface. It shouldn't take you long to get used to the new design and once you know a few tricks, I think you'll actually prefer the new environment.

Many general tasks remain unchanged in the new version of Photoshop. You can still move, rearrange and collapse the panels down to an icon using the same general methods used in the past. Here's a list of what's changed in CS4:

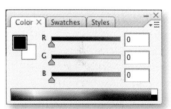

Photoshop CS3 style Tab Group.

Photoshop CS4 Tab Group.

Collapse Tab Group: You'll no longer find the collapse icon "−" in the upper right of a panel. You'll instead need to double-click on any of the tabs to collapse the panel.

Close Tabs: In previous versions you were able to close a single tab by clicking on the "**X**" that appeared next to its name or close an entire group of tabs by clicking the "**X**" that was found in the upper right corner of the group. That's no longer the case. You now have to choose the appropriate command from the side menu of each tab group. This is a much less efficient process, but they did clean up the appearance of the tab groups in the process.

Close
Close Tab Group

Reposition Tabs: The gray bar that used to appear above each tab group now only appears when the tab group is not docked to other tab groups. That means you'll have to drag from the empty space to the right of the tabs in order to reposition the entire tab group. Dragging on the dark gray bar that appears at the top of vertically stacked tab groups will move the entire stack. That wasn't possible in previous versions.

Icon Mode: You can collapse any panel or tab group into an icon by clicking on the double arrow that appears in the upper right of the tab group. That functionality is not new, but you can now drag a panel icon and place it below the Tool bar or put it on top of the Options or Application bars that are found at the top of your screen. I always use the empty space below the Tool bar to store panels that don't get a lot of use (like the Swatches, Styles and Clone Source panels). That way all those panels are only a click away and they don't take up any extra space on my screen.

Application Bar

Adobe has added a new feature to all the applications in the Creative Suite (Illustrator, InDesign, etc.) that's known as the Application bar. This new bar appears at the top of your screen just above the familiar Options bar and is combined with the menu bar on Windows, but not on the Mac. For Mac users, the new bar is a little bit of a rebel in that you can dock it below or above the Options bar, but you can't dock it into the empty gray space in the Options bar (only float above it), which would be an obvious place for it. Again for Mac users, you can toggle the visibility of this bar by choosing **Window>Application Bar**. (Note: the toggle feature doesn't work when the Application Frame—which I'll discuss later in this chapter—is in use.) From left to right, this is what you'll find in the new Application bar:

Application Icon: The icon on the far left of the Application bar simply identifies which application you are running within the Creative Suite.

Bridge Icon: Clicking this icon will launch Bridge and bring it to the front so you can browse your images.

Extras Menu: Clicking this icon will produce a drop-down menu that allows you to show or hide guides, grids or rulers.

Magnification Menu: Clicking on the percentage symbol shown in the Application bar will allow you to zoom in or out on your image to preset magnifications.

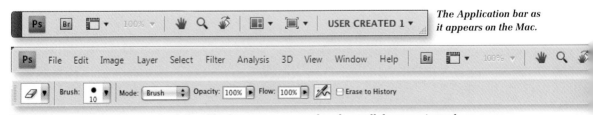

The Application bar as it appears on the Mac.

The Options bar extends across the full width of your screen even though not all the space is used.

Navigation Tools: Continuing to the right on the Application bar, you'll find  copies of the **Hand** and **Zoom** tools along with the new **Rotate View** tool, which we'll discuss in Chapter 5.

Arrange Documents Menu: This menu allows you to change the layout of your screen when multiple documents are open. The upper left icon will consolidate all the open documents into a single tabbed window (we'll discuss tabbed windows in more detail later in this chapter). The other icons in the top row will tile the open documents into an equal number of rows and columns (vertical or horizontal) to make it easier to compare their contents. The icons shown below the first row offer various window layouts that limit the number of documents that will fit the screen (like two up, three up, and so on). The number of layout icons available will depend on the number of your open images.

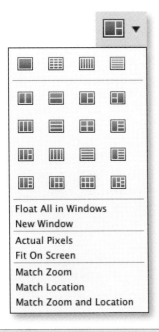

The Application bar in Windows.

Once you have chosen a layout that works for your purposes, you can choose **Match Zoom** to make sure the documents are all being viewed at the same magnification, or choose **Match Location** to view the same area in each document (assuming the documents contain similar content, are the same size and that you've zoomed into a specific area in the active document that you want to inspect in the others).

> **NOTE**
>
> **Multi-Window Control**
> *Hold the **Shift** key when using the **Hand** tool or **Zoom** tool to navigate all open documents at the same time.*

The other choices found in the **Arrange Documents** pop-up menu are also found under the **Window** and **View** menus, including one option that is new to Photoshop CS4: **Float All in Windows** (which we'll discuss when we talk about **Tabbed Documents** later in this chapter).

Screen Mode Menu: This menu is not new to Photoshop. It used to be found at the bottom of the Tool bar and has simply been moved to this new position. You'll find that the **Maximized Screen Mode** they added in Photoshop CS3 has been removed in CS4. (It was a mode that prevented docked palettes from covering up the image and provided scroll bars for times when the image extended beyond the edge of the monitor.) I'm still befuddled as to why they went to the trouble of adding that screen mode in the previous version if they were going to simply remove it from the next.

Workspace Menu: You'll find the **Workspace** menu on the far right of the Application bar. This is not a new feature. In Photoshop CS3, the workspace menu was located near the right end of the Options bar.

Now that you're familiar with the new Application bar, let's explore what they've changed in the area of viewing and navigating between documents.

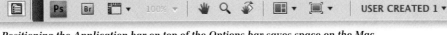

Positioning the Application bar on top of the Options bar saves space on the Mac.

Tabbed Windows

Photoshop CS4 allows you to display multiple documents as tabs in a single window. This concept is identical to what you will find in most modern web browsers. It's a great new feature that can go a long way toward keeping your workspace neat and clean, and the nice thing is that it gives you complete flexibility in that you can pull a document out of the tabbed window, or turn off the feature altogether in Preferences. Let's take a look at the mechanics of working with tabbed windows.

A single window containing multiple documents being displayed as tabs.

Creating Tabs: Photoshop CS4 will use tabbed windows by default. All you have to do is either open multiple images, or create multiple documents from scratch. As you open or create more and more images, they will appear in a single window under tabs that display the file name of each document.

Floating a Window: The process of pulling a document out of a tabbed window and into one of its own is known as "floating the window," and there are a number of ways to do it. You can drag a tab to an open area of your screen or choose **Window>Arrange>Float in Window**. Another option, similar to how tabbed web browsers operate, is to **Control-click** (Mac) or **Right-click** (Win) on the tab and select **Move to New Window**. You

can choose **Float All in Windows** from the same menu to get all the open documents to appear in separate windows.

Multiple Tabbed Windows: You can also have multiple windows, each containing their own set of tabs. To accomplish that, open multiple images, drag a tab out of the tabbed window to create a second window and then drag additional tabs onto the newly created window. Once you have multiple tabbed windows, you can drag the title bar of a tabbed window to move all the tabs within that window.

If you change your mind and would like all open documents to be displayed in a single tabbed window, choose **Window>Arrange>Consolidate All to Tabs** or use the top left icon in the **Arrange Documents** menu that was covered earlier in this chapter.

Changing Tab Order: Simply drag individual tabs right or left to change the order in which they appear across the top of a window.

Navigating Tabbed Windows: Click on the name of any tab to make it display its contents. You can also type **Control-Tab** to cycle through the tabs (add **Shift** to go back instead of forward). Adobe has also enabled the standard Mac keyboard shortcut to cycle through open windows which is **Command-~**. Photoshop will always cycle through the tabs in the order the documents were opened (which might not corollate to the order the tabs are in at the moment you use these keyboard shortcuts).

If there are too many tabs open to be displayed in the space available, a double arrow icon will appear to the right of the tabs. Clicking on that icon will present you with a list of all documents that are contained within the window. Choosing a document from the menu will make its tab active.

If a window is too small to display all the tabs it contains, a double arrow icon will appear on its right edge.

Preventing Tab Creation: If you find that you really don't like the concept of tabbed windows and are nostalgic for the way earlier versions of Photoshop worked, you're in luck. Adobe has added two new preferences to the **Interface** section of the **Preferences** dialog box, which is found under the **Photoshop** menu (Mac), or **Edit** menu (Win). Turning off the **Open Documents as Tabs** checkbox will prevent Photoshop from automatically using tabs when you open a document or create a new one. Turning off the **Enable Floating Document Window Docking** checkbox (that's a mouthful) will prevent you from being able to create tabs by dragging between windows.

☑ Open Documents as Tabs
☑ Enable Floating Document Window Docking

The two settings shown above are found in the Interface section of Photoshop's Preferences dialog box.

The Ultimate Solution: You don't have to commit one way or the other. You can always hold the **Control** key (on Mac or Win) while dragging the title bar of a window to temporarily toggle the **Enable Floating Document Window Docking** preference. If you have the preference turned off, it will allow you to create tabs, and if the preference is turned on, then holding **Control** will prevent you from creating a tab.

My personal choice is to turn off both of the preferences I mentioned above and simply drag while holding **Control** anytime I want to create a tab. Or, I will use the various menu choices I mentioned earlier when I need to consolidate a large number of documents into a single window.

Application Frame

Windows users are accustomed to having their panels, documents and other Photoshop elements contained within a medium gray backdrop that obscures their view of items that are located on their desktop. Mac users on the other hand, often have to deal with a lot more clutter since they can easily see all the items on their desktop along with any other running applications. In Photoshop CS4, you can choose **Window>Application Frame** to get a similar gray backdrop on the Mac. I'll refer to this feature as either the Application Frame or simply the backdrop since there really isn't any sort of a "frame" around its edge.

The new Application Frame places a medium gray backdrop behind all your documents.

When you turn that setting on, any panels that were docked to the edge of your screen will now be attached to the edge of the backdrop. You can resize the backdrop by dragging its lower right corner. You can also make the frame fill your screen (if it isn't already) by clicking on the green icon (which I think of as a jellybean) that's displayed in the upper left of the frame window.

I find that this Application Frame is very useful when teaching hands-on training classes to Windows users in a classroom full of Macs (which is often the case in many graphic arts related training centers). Windows users often get disoriented when they accidently click on their desktop, which causes it to become active, therefore hiding all of Photoshop's panels. With the new Application Frame, Photoshop's panels will still be visible when you switch to another program.

If you're a die-hard Mac user, you might find this new mode to be rather odd since no other program acts this way.

Miscellaneous Changes

Flash Extensions

Adobe has given third parties (like plug-in developers) the ability to create their own panels using Adobe Flash. That means we'll no longer be limited to adding extra functionality to Photoshop through plug-in filters. I look forward to seeing what the third-party folks come up with in the months after the product ships (no announcements have been made at press time).

Photoshop CS4 ships with two Flash Extensions. You can access them from the **Window>Extensions** menu. We'll discuss the new **Kuler** and **Connections** extensions that come with Photoshop CS4 in Chapter 7.

Interface Preferences

There have been a few changes in the **Interface** section of Photoshop's **Preferences** dialog box (which you can access via the **Photoshop** menu on a Mac or the **Edit** menu in Windows).

Full Screen Settings: Starting at the top of the dialog box, you'll find new settings to specify which color background you'd like to have when using full screen mode (via the new pop-up menu found in the Application bar). Those settings are not new since you could always **Control-click** (Mac), or **Right-click** (Win) on the surround color when in full screen mode to change it. They've

simply moved those settings into the **Preferences** dialog box to make them a little easier to find. The **Border** setting is new and allows you to choose the style of effect you'd like to have added to the edge of your documents (which helps indicate where the document ends and the full screen mode color begins).

UI Language: This new setting allows you to specify the language used to display all of Photoshop's interface elements. Most users will only have once choice available in this menu, but additional languages should eventually be available from Adobe.

Auto-Show Hidden Panels: With this option turned on, you can press **Tab** to hide all visible panels and then move your mouse to the edge of your screen to make panels that were touching the edge of your screen visible. Moving your mouse away from the edge of your screen will cause the panels to become hidden once again.

As you can see, Adobe is working hard to redefine Photoshop (they claim for the greater good of the entire Creative Suite), and the souped-up interface is a big part of that effort. With one glaring exception (the use of that wretched word, "panel") and a few minor ones, I'm finding that the majority of improvements are just that, improvements. There weren't any major stumbles in the CS4 interface— I absolutely love the new tabbed windows option—and I suggest that before trying to turn everything off in Preferences, you give it a good chance, devote some time to it, and it won't be long before you feel just as protective of these new features as you did your favorites in previous versions of Photoshop.

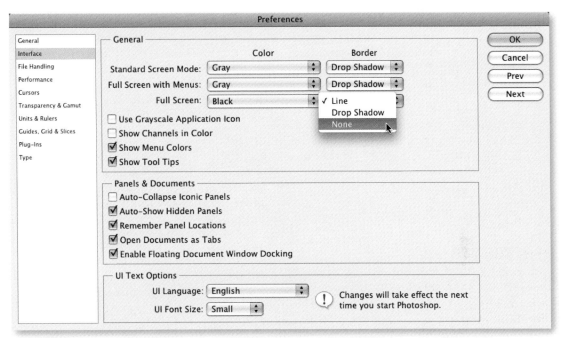

Choose Preferences>Interface from the Photoshop menu (Mac), or Edit menu (Win) to access these settings.

Chapter 4
Adjustments

THE OVERALL ADJUSTMENT INTERFACE IN Photoshop CS4 is a radical departure from earlier versions. If you're willing to work with Adjustment Layers (and if you're not, shame on you), your world will be forever changed as you find yourself liberated from the modal hell that has imprisoned Photoshop users for over a decade.

Below is an overview of what we'll be covering in this chapter:

- **Adjustments Panel:** For those of you using Adjustment Layers, this new panel is command central for your adjustment activity. Unlike the traditional Adjustment Layer interface, this panel is not modal (a dialog box that pops up and while open prevents you from accessing any other operation inside the application). This means that all of Photoshop's features are now at your disposal even while you're in the middle of adjusting your images. All I can say is....free at last!.
- **Vibrance Adjustment:** Snagged from Camera Raw, this adjustment makes its debut in Photoshop CS4. It's especially useful for boosting skin tone without over-saturating.
- **Targeted Adjustment Icon:** A new icon has been added to some adjustments that allows you to click and drag on your image to quickly isolate and adjust an area.
- **Misc. Changes:** We'll look at the less obvious changes hidden within the CS4 upgrade such as the new pop-up menu shortcuts and additional adjustment presets.

Where's My Stuff?

The world of adjustments has largely been turned on its head. Here's what's happened to many of the features you've depended on for years:

- **Auto Levels:** The **Auto Levels** adjustment has been renamed **Auto Tone** and has been moved to the **Image** menu.
- **Automated Adjustments:** If you're searching for any of the automated adjustments such as **Auto Tone**, **Auto Contrast** and **Auto Color**, you'll have to look in the main **Image** menu without going to the **Adjustments** submenu.
- **Adjustment Layers:** You're going to be in a foreign land when you go to use Adjustment Layers in CS4. The adjustment dialog boxes have been replaced with the new **Adjustments** panel. Make sure to read this chapter to get acclimated to the new environment.
- **Levels Options:** If you're looking for the **Options** button in a **Levels** Adjustment Layer, you'll now find it—renamed **Auto Options**—in the side menu of the **Adjustments** panel.

- **Curves Options:** For Adjustment Layers,  the choices that were accessed from **Curve Display Options** near the bottom of the **Curves** dialog box are now found in the side menu of the **Curves** adjustment panel, as are the **Auto Color Correction Options** that were accessed by clicking the Options button located on the right side of the **Curves** dialog box. The standard **Curves** dialog box (non-adjustment layer) remains unchanged.

- **Channel Shortcuts:** Holding **Command** (Mac), or **Ctrl** (Win) and typing number keys will no longer switch the channel you're editing in Levels, Curves or other adjustments. You will have to instead hold the **Option** key (Mac), or **Alt** key (Win) and type a number, but the number will be two higher than you're used to. So, if you used to type **Command-1** to get to the Red channel, you'll now have to type **Option-3** to do the same thing.

- **Tabbing Through Curves Points:** In Photoshop CS3, you could type **Control-Tab** (Mac or Win) to cycle through points on a curve. You now have to press the **Plus** or **Minus** keys (without **Shift** being held down) to do the same in CS4.

- **Tint in Black & White:** The Hue and Saturation sliders that were found in the **Black & White** adjustment dialog box have been replaced by a color swatch which produces the Color Picker. You can still enter **Hue** and **Saturation** values, or you can choose a hue from the vertical bar and then drag horizontally within the large color field to change the **Saturation** setting.

- **Presets Pop-Up Menu:** The icon found next to the presets pop-up menu that used to be found at the top of many adjustment dialog boxes has been replaced by choices that are now found on the side menu of the new **Adjustments** panel.

Adjustments Panel

The dialog boxes used for adjusting images in all previous versions of Photoshop have been modal. Once you started to edit an adjustment, you were in "adjustment mode" and most of Photoshop's interface was not available. This made for some frustrating times when you wanted to perform simple tasks, such as changing the **Blending Mode** via the pop-up menu at the top of the **Layers** panel, painting on the mask attached to an Adjustment Layer, or clipping the adjustment to an underlying layer. The process went something like this:

1) Create an Adjustment Layer and start to darken your image only to notice that it's becoming too colorful.
2) Click **OK** in the adjustment dialog box to gain access to the rest of Photoshop's interface and change the **Blending Mode** pop-up menu to **Luminosity** to prevent color changes.
3) Double-click the thumbnail for the Adjustment Layer to return to adjusting your image.
4) After fine-tuning the adjustment, you decide that you want to limit the areas that are being darkened.
5) Click **OK** (again) in the adjustment dialog box to gain access to the features in the **Layers** panel and then paint on the mask attached to the Adjustment Layer to prevent the adjustment from affecting the entire image.
6) Now that you've limited the adjustment to a particular layer, you decide that you can get away with darkening the image even more. So, you double-click the thumbnail for the Adjustment Layer to return to adjusting your image.
7) Forget why you were adjusting the image in the first place because you've been mentally distracted by having to work around the annoying modal state of the adjustment dialog box one too many times.
8) Repeat the above process dozens (if not hundreds) of times a day and watch your hair slowly fall out of your head and fall on the floor.

Photoshop CS4's new **Adjustments** panel frees us from the modal hell that has plagued us for over a decade. You won't fully grasp just how liberating this new feature is until you've worked with it long enough to have its newness rub off. That's when you'll realize that adjustments in Photoshop have become so unbelievably easy, it feels as natural to make an adjustment as it does to take your next breath.

NOTE

Modal Adjustments
*The new **Adjustments** panel is only used when applying an adjustment as an Adjustment Layer. Adjusting a layer directly by choosing from the **Image>Adjustments** menu will present you with the old-style dialog boxes that lock out most of Photoshop's functionality. Adjustment Layers are a much more versatile way to apply an adjustment.*

before continuing to read this section. You can learn about them in my book, *Adobe Photoshop Studio Techniques*, or any number of free online Photoshop resources.

For those of you familiar with Adjustment Layers, you now have three choices for creating one: **1)** Choose from the **Layer>New Adjustment Layer** menu, **2)** Choose from the **Adjustment Layer** pop-up menu at the bottom of the **Layers** panel, or **3)** Choose from the new **Adjustments** panel. Let's take a look at the new **Adjustment** panel and see how it will change your workflow.

Adjustment Icons

The new **Adjustments** panel should be visible when you first launch Photoshop CS4. If you don't see it on your screen, choose **Window>Adjustments**.

You'll find 15 icons at the top of the **Adjustments** panel, one for each type of Adjustment Layer you can create. Clicking on one of those icons will create a brand new Adjustment Layer and fill the **Adjustment** panel with the controls related to the adjustment you are applying. If you have trouble translating which icon represents which adjustment, just hover over the icon and a tool tip will appear that indicates the type of adjustment that would be created if you clicked on that icon. You can also see what the icon represents via a text label that appears just below the panel's title tab "Adjustments." This is even faster than the hovering technique.

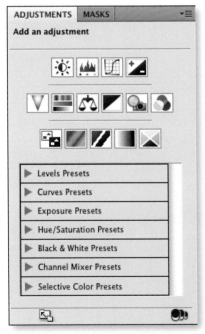

Photoshop CS4's new Adjustments panel. An arrow will appear at the bottom of the panel when an Adjustment Layer is active. Clicking the icon will switch between the adjustment controls and the adjustment icons used to create a new Adjustment Layer.

ADJUSTMENT ICONS	
Name	Icon
Brightness|Contrast	
Levels	
Curves	
Exposure	
Vibrance	
Hue/Saturation	
Color Balance	
Black & White	
Photo Filter	
Channel Mixer	
Invert	
Posterize	
Threshold	
Gradient Map	
Selective Color	

For you folks who don't use Adjustment Layers (which is what is created when using the new Adjustments panel), you're truly missing out on the best that Photoshop has to offer, so I suggest you stop whatever you're doing immediately, and take a few minutes to get familiar with them

Modal Versus Non-Modal Adjustments

Here are the adjustment dialog boxes that were formerly available as Adjustment Layers and the Adjustment panels that have replaced them. Most options that do not appear in the panels (like the options at the bottom of Curves) are available from their side menus.

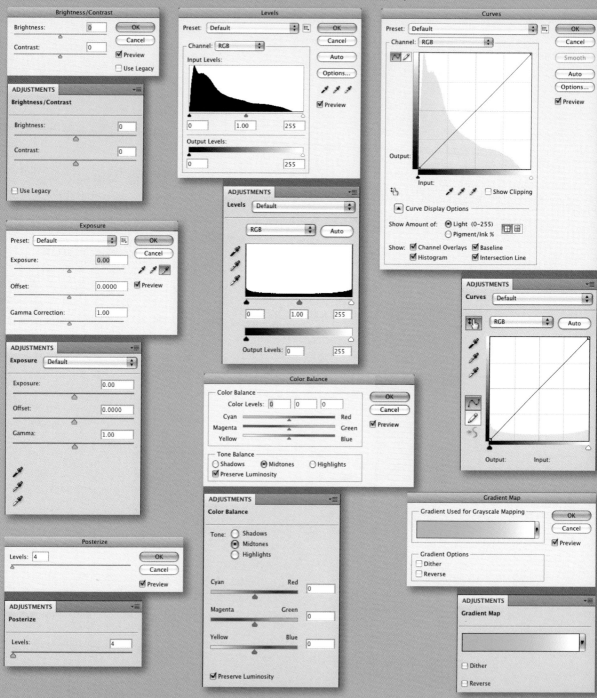

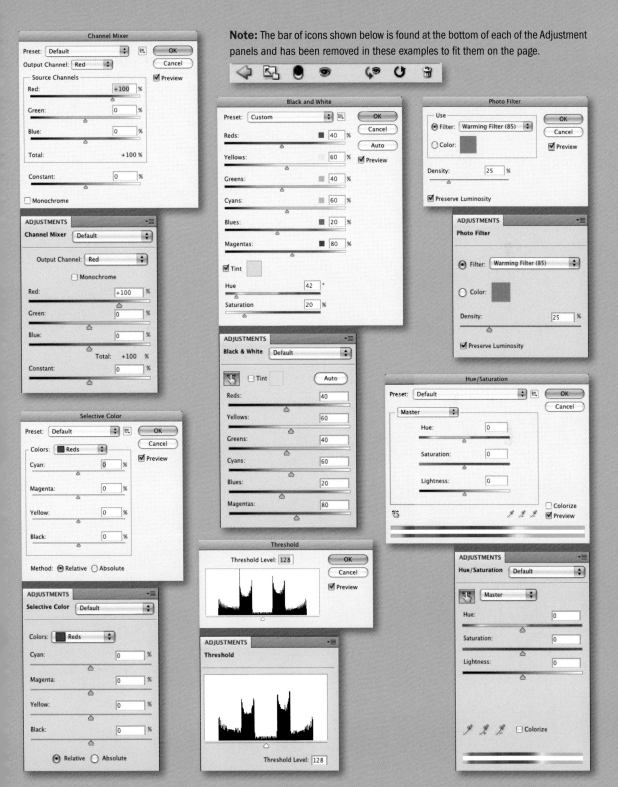

Note: The bar of icons shown below is found at the bottom of each of the Adjustment panels and has been removed in these examples to fit them on the page.

Presets List

You'll find a list of presets below the adjustment icons. A single click on one of the presets will create a new Adjustment Layer with those settings attached to it.

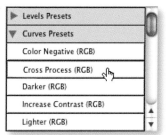

The adjustment preset list.

A wider variety of adjustments have presets available in CS4 (like Hue/Saturation for instance) and the list of presets for many of the adjustments has been expanded from what was available in the previous version of Photoshop.

To create your own preset, choose **Save Preset** from the side menu of the **Adjustments** panel while you are editing an adjustment. You can also switch the preset you are applying by choosing from the pop-up menu that appears at the top of any adjustment panel.

Adjustments Panel

Once you've clicked on one of the adjustment icons or chosen from the presets list, the content of the **Adjustments** panel will change to present you with the controls related to the adjustment you have chosen.

While editing an adjustment, you are free to use all the features in Photoshop. That means that you can easily change the **Blending Mode** menu at the top of the **Layers** panel, lower the opacity of the layer, paint on the mask attached to the layer, make selections, and much more.

At the bottom of the **Adjustments** panel, you'll find seven icons. Let's take a look at what each one is for:

Toggle List/Adjustment: When an Adjustment Layer is active, an arrow icon will appear in the lower left corner of the **Adjustments** panel. Clicking the icon will toggle you between the the list of adjustment icons and presets and the adjustment controls related to the active Adjustment Layer. That icon is useful when you're done performing an adjustment and would like to create a new Adjustment Layer.

Standard/Expanded: Clicking this icon, which looks like a tiny file folder with an arrow etched on top, will toggle between the standard-sized adjustment panel and the wider expanded version. It doesn't add any functionality to the adjustments, but it is useful if you find the default **Curves** dialog box to be a bit cramped.

Clip to Layer: This icon, which looks like two circles overlapping, allows you to clip the active Adjustment Layer to the underlying layer. If the layer below contains an image, the adjustment will only affect the contents of that layer. If the underlying layer contains an adjustment, then the mask attached to that layer will also affect the active Adjustment Layer.

You'll find a similar icon at the bottom of the **Adjustments** panel when viewing the adjustment icons and preset list. Clicking that icon will toggle it on or off, which will cause any future adjustments you create to automatically be clipped to the underlying layer.

You can tell that two or more layers are part of a clipping group when a down-pointing arrow appears next the Adjustment Layer.

Visibility: The eye icon will toggle the visibility of the Adjustment Layer to show you what your image would look like with and without the Adjustment Layer. This icon is identical in function to the one that appears next to each Adjustment Layer in the **Layers** panel.

Previous State: The icon with the little eye 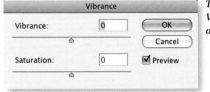 and curved arrow allows you to see what your image looked like before you started to edit the current Adjustment Layer. If you've switched to a different layer and back to an Adjustment Layer and then started to edit the adjustment, this icon will show you what the Adjustment Layer looked like before you started to modify the adjustment. You can temporarily invoke this preview by holding the / key on your keyboard. The Previous State view will remain on for as long as you hold down that key.

Defaults/Reset State: The next icon, which looks like a circular shaped arrow, will change appearance, looking like a full circle if you're working on a newly created Adjustment Layer or a half circle if you're re-editing an existing Adjustment Layer. Clicking on the icon in its first state will reset the adjustment dialog box to its default settings, which is the same as deleting the Adjustment Layer and starting the adjustment from scratch. In its second, half-circle state, the icon will undo any changes you've made since you started to re-edit the adjustment. Both of these icons only affect changes made to the adjustment itself and will not affect changes to the **Opacity** or **Blending Mode** at the top of the **Layers** panel.

Delete Adjustment: Clicking the trash icon will delete the active Adjustment Layer.

Now that you are familiar with the icons at the bottom of the **Adjustments** panel, let's take a look at a few more Adjustment Layer-related features that are new in Photoshop CS4

Adjustment Options: You can access the options for a layer at the moment you're creating an Adjustment Layer by holding the **Option** key (Mac), or **Alt** key (Win) and clicking on one of the adjustment icons in the **Adjustments** panel.

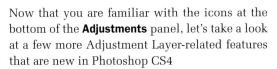

Edit Adjustment Menu: You'll find a new **Edit Adjustment** option when **Control-clicking** (Mac), or **Right-clicking** (Win) on an Adjustment Layer in the **Layers** panel. The same choice is also available from the side menu of the **Layers** panel. This is a convenient way to get the **Adjustments** panel to appear if it's not currently visible on your screen.

Photoshop CS4 also features a new **Masks** panel that is very useful when working with Adjustment Layers. Since it's useful when working with any type of layer, we'll talk about that feature in Chapter 6-Layers.

Now let's take a look at the changes they've made to specific adjustments in Photoshop.

Vibrance Adjustment

Adobe has taken the **Vibrance** adjustment that was only available in Adobe Camera Raw and incorporated it into Photoshop CS4. It is available both as a direct adjustment (via the **Image>Adjustments** menu) and as an Adjustment Layer.

When you adjust an image using the new Vibrance adjustment, you'll be presenting with two sliders: **Vibrance** and **Saturation**.

The new Vibrance adjustment.

Saturation

The **Saturation** slider is the same as the one you'll find in the **Hue/Saturation** dialog box. Moving it toward the left will make your image less colorful, while moving it to the right will make your image more colorful.

The problem with the **Saturation** slider is that it treats all colors equally. That means one color can easily become overly saturated before another reaches its full potential. Just think about a pho-

Top Left: Original.

Top Right: Saturation increased (clipping),

Left: Vibrance increased instead (no clipping).

tograph of a flower. If you were to increase the saturation of the entire image, you might oversaturate the flower before the brown soil it's planted in becomes as colorful as you desire. If you push the **Saturation** slider until the soil reaches its full potential, the much more colorful flower will become oversaturated and look artificial. When an area becomes oversaturated, it starts to lose detail, which is known as *Saturation Clipping*.

> ### NOTE
>
> **Saturation Clipping**
>
> *Losing detail in the more colorful area of an image by over saturating the image is known as **Saturation Clipping**.*
>
> *To have full detail in an area, you need detail in all three of the channels that make up your image. As you increase saturation it has the effect of increasing the contrast of the three channels (RGB) that make up your image. If you push the slider far enough, you will cause the brightest and/ or darkest areas in one or two of the channels to become "clipped" to solid white or solid black. Clipping one or more channels has the effect of reducing detail.*

Vibrance

This adjustment was invented in an effort to prevent saturation clipping. The **Vibrance** slider works just like the **Saturation** slider in that it makes your image more or less colorful. The difference is that the **Vibrance** slider will boost the saturation of the areas that are not all that colorful a lot more than the areas that are already colorful. If you think back to our flower example, increasing the **Vibrance** would make the soil much more colorful while only affecting the flower a small amount.

Original image.

The **Vibrance** slider also attempts to prevent skin tones from becoming overly colorful (which might cause people to look sunburned).

For the reasons stated above, many people have completely replaced the **Saturation** slider with the **Vibrance** slider. I suggest you use them together in the following ways:

Exaggerate Mellow Colors: If you want the not-so-colorful areas of your image to stand out, consider lowering the **Saturation** setting while increasing the **Vibrance** setting. On some images, I'll even crank the **Vibrance** slider all the way to the right and then lower the **Saturation** slider until the image doesn't look overly colorful.

Tone Down Mellow Colors: Sometimes you'll want the most colorful areas to be center stage and not be distracted by surrounding elements. That's when I'll move the **Vibrance** slider down quite a bit (sometimes all the way to -100) and then adjust the **Saturation** slider until the more color-ful areas within the image look appropriate.

Most of the time I use one of the above approaches and simply don't take it to the extreme I've shown in these examples.

Result of reducing vibrance.

Result of increasing vibrance.

Settings used to produce the result shown above.

Settings used to produce the result shown above.

Targeted Adjustments

The new **Targeted Adjustment** icon (which looks like a tiny hand next to a two-headed arrow) has been added to the **Curves**, **Hue/Saturation** and **Black & White** adjustments. It allows you to click and drag within your image to quickly isolate and adjust areas. Being able to isolate areas is not new to these adjustments; this icon simply allows for faster interaction with the image compared to previous versions of Photoshop. Clicking the icon will toggle it on or off (it's off by default). Let's look at how it works with each of the adjustments in which it's available:

Curves

In Curves, you used to have to hold the **Command** key (Mac), or **Ctrl** key (Win) and click within your image (which is still possible) to measure the brightness of an area and add a point to the appropriate area of the curve that would concentrate an adjustment on that area. You'd then have to move your mouse into the **Curves** dialog box and drag the newly added point up or down to brighten or darken the area. At the same time you'd have to be very careful not to accidently move the point horizontally, otherwise it would no longer correspond to the brightness of the area you clicked on within your image. Many people preferred to use the **Up/Down Arrow** keys instead of their mouse just to avoid moving a point horizontally.

When the new **Targeted Adjustment** icon is active, all you have to do to add a point to the curve is to click within your image. To adjust the newly added point, simply drag up or down within your image. There is no need to release the mouse button—this can be one fluid motion, and you don't have to worry about dragging horizontally since that doesn't affect the movement of the curve point.

This simple change might not sound all that ground-breaking, but when combined with the new **Adjustments** panel, it can almost infinitely speed up how quickly you can adjust an image. The old method feels like trying to unlock your car using a coat hanger through a closed window instead of simply grabbing for the key and unlocking the door directly.

Hue/Saturation

In previous versions of Photoshop, you had to choose a color from the pop-up menu at the top of the **Hue/Saturation** dialog box to isolate a color and then click within your image to focus an adjustment on a specific color within your image. After doing that, you could adjust the **Hue**, **Saturation** or **Lightness** sliders to change the look of the area. If you had to change more than one color within your image, you'd have to choose a different color from the pop-up menu, click on another area within your image and then adjust the sliders once again.

When the new **Drag to Adjust** icon is active, all you have to do is click on the color you'd like to change and then drag horizontally to adjust the **Saturation** slider. If you want to adjust a second area, just move your mouse over the second color and drag away. If you need to change the **Hue** slider, hold down the **Command** key (Mac), or **Ctrl** key (Win) as you drag. With any of these adjustments, you can add the **Shift** key to make more dramatic changes to your image, or hold **Option** (Mac), or **Alt** (Win) to make finer adjustments. The only bummer about this method is that you have to manually adjust the **Lightness** slider because there is no modifier key that allows you to drag on your image and affect the **Lightness** slider.

Black & White

The **Drag to Adjust** icon doesn't add any new functionality to the Black & White adjustment —since you were able to click and drag on the image in Photoshop CS3—but having the icon available simply makes that feature a little more accessible. Oh, well.

Misc. Changes

Now that's you've seen most of the major adjustment-related changes in CS4, let's take a look at some of the less visible alterations.

Pop-Up Menu Shortcuts: Some of the keyboard shortcuts you may be accustomed to using when applying an adjustment have changed. When Adobe started moving away from the modal design of Adjustment Layers, they needed to make sure that any keyboard shortcuts that were specific to an adjustment did not interfere with the ones used by the other features in Photoshop.

A big conflict arose when it came to holding **Command** (Mac) or **Ctrl** (Win) and typing a number, a shortcut already being used to view various channels in the **Channels** panel. That same shortcut was used in adjustment dialog boxes to target (not view) a particular channel, so they needed to make a change. You now hold the **Option** key (Mac), or **Alt** key (Win) and type a number to choose a channel within adjustments like Levels and Curves. The numbers you type will also be off by two. Meaning that if you're accustomed to using the number 1 to get to the red channel, you'll now have to use the number 3 for the same task.

More Adjustments Have Presets: It's now possible to create and use presets with Levels and Hue/Saturation adjustments. That also means that two new folders have been added to the **Photoshop>Presets** directory on your hard drive to accompany those new presets.

Histogram Defaults: Adobe has changed the default setting for the **Histogram** panel so that it more closely reflects the look of histograms found in Adobe Camera Raw and Lightroom. The histogram now displays an overlay of the red, green and blue channels that make up your image.

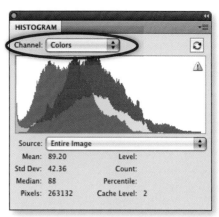

The default setting for the Channel pop-up menu in the Histogram panel has been changed from RGB to Colors.

If you prefer the old look of the Histogram panel, choose **Expanded View** from the side menu of the panel and change the **Channel** pop-up menu at the top of the panel to RGB.

That's it for my coverage of the new adjustment features in CS4. Each new version of Photoshop brings with it a standout feature that truly advances the evolution of the program and dramatically improves the overall experience of working with it. For many (including me), this feature will be the new **Adjustments** panel. Being able to get away from those the traditional, straightjacket-style modal dialog boxes is like being able to play the piano with both hands, instead of with one tied behind your back. Mind you, there are still plenty of those crusty, old dialog boxes lurking in many other corners of Photoshop, but ain't it grand to have a place to get away from them?

Chapter 5
Tools

T HE CS4 TOOL REFINEMENTS ALONE might be responsible for saving the global Photoshop community literally billions of hours of clicking, mousing and maneuvering. It wasn't just the Zoom tool that got the zoom treatment; some of Photoshop's most essential tools just got a heck of a lot more efficient and intuitive.

Below is an overview of what we'll be covering in this chapter.

- **Brushes:** There are new, time-saving methods for resizing your brushes, and the painting action is now a much more fluid experience.
- **Retouching Tools:** Several modifications made to the **Dodge**, **Burn**, **Clone** and **Healing Brush** tools make them much more useful.
- **Note Tool:** See how the **Note** tool has grown up and become more practical for real-world users, even getting its own **Notes** panel so you can review multiple notes without having to face an obstacle course of little Note icons cluttering your image.
- **Rotate View Tool:** You can now view your images at an angle without actually rotating the pixels that make up the image.
- **Navigation Methods:** There are all sorts of new ways to pan and zoom around your images, some of which feel turbo-charged.
- **Misc. Changes:** Discover all the small changes that have been made to the tools including the new spring-loaded keyboard shortcuts and new **Eyedropper** tool options.

Where's My Stuff?

When it comes to the tools update in CS4, very little was done that might cause disorientation:

- **Audio Annotation Tool:** The **Audio Annotation** tool was sent packing, but its cousin, the **Note** tool, got a slick CS4 makeover, as well as a new location in the **Tool** bar, where it shares a space with the **Eyedropper** tool.
- **Cloning Overlay:** If you're used to holding **Shift-Option** (Mac), or **Shift-Alt** (Win) to see a preview when using the cloning tools, you'll find that shortcut works differently in CS4. To get back to the old behavior, you can change the following settings: turn off the **Show Overlay** and **Clipped** checkboxes in the **Clone Source** panel, turn on the **Invert** checkbox, and set the **Opacity** to 50%.
- **Retouching Cursors:** If you don't like the new in-cursor cloning preview, you can turn off the **Show Overlay** and **Clipped** checkboxes in the **Clone Source** panel.
- **Slice Tools:** If you're searching for the **Slice** and **Slice Selection** tools, take a look in the same slot as the **Crop** tool.

Brushes

There have been a few changes to how brushes work in CS4—none too terribly radical—but all quite welcome.

Enhanced Cursors

Brush cursors now feature a glowing edge to make them stand out from any background. This enhancement was added without degrading performance because Adobe off-loaded much of the work to your video card's Graphics Processing Unit (GPU). It's too bad they didn't do the same with the selection tools. The **Marquee** crosshair cursor still virtually disappears on 50% gray backgrounds and is in desperate need of some cursor enhancement. Maybe next time.

Left: Photoshop CS3's brush cursor. Right: CS4's new brush cursor features a glowing edge.

Drag-Resizing Brushes

You can now change the **Diameter** or **Hardness** setting of a brush by dragging your mouse. This is wonderfully liberating for situations when you need to frequently change the settings of your brush (retouching tasks come to mind) because it allows you to keep your right hand on your mouse (or graphics tablet) without having the constant interruption of switching to the bracket keys on your keyboard, or having to mouse your way over to the **Brush Preset** panel.

To change the **Diameter** of your brush, use the following mouse/keyboard combinations: On the Mac, drag your mouse while holding down the **Control** and **Option** keys. On Windows, hold the **Alt** key and use the right mouse button when dragging.

These examples show you what you can expect to see while using the techniques mentioned above.

To change the **Hardness** setting of your brush, use these mouse and keyboard combinations: On the Mac, drag the mouse while holding the **Control**, **Option** and **Command** keys. On Windows, press the right mouse button and drag while holding down the **Alt** and **Shift** keys. While dragging, you will see a red circle that will give you a preview of the brush settings. You might find yourself having to drag outside the document window to reach the maximum or minimum setting. For instance, in testing this feature I had to drag my cursor way beyond the document window to reach 100% **Hardness**.

Example brush previews created while changing the Hardness setting of a brush.

The color of the brush resize preview is determined by the **Brush Preview** setting that's found in the **Cursors** section of Photoshop's **Preferences** dialog box.

Clicking the color swatch will produce a color picker that allows you to change the color used for the brush resize preview.

Many of the changes made to the brush cursors rely on your computer's video card. You might find that these features are not available when using a vintage computer that doesn't have an up-to-date video card.

With the addition of drag-resizing, you now have four options for resizing your brush. Here are your options and an accompanying example of when I would use them:

Brushes Panel: Accessed via the **Window** menu or by clicking the **Brush** icon in the **Options** bar (which will change appearance depending on which tool is active). I use this option when I need to change individual settings for a brush such as **Scattering**, **Texture** and more.

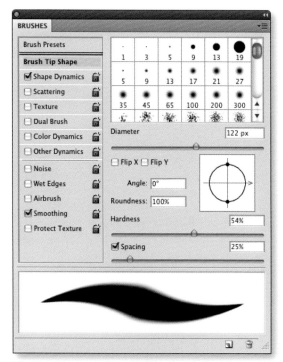

The Brushes panel allows full access to all of the parameters that define a brush.

Brush Presets Panel: Accessed by clicking on the brush preview that's found near the left edge of the **Options** bar when any painting or retouching tool is active. I use this option when I need to access unusually shaped brushes that have already been defined as a preset (you can only create presets in the full **Brushes** panel). Otherwise, I find this to be a cumbersome method for changing the **Diameter** or **Hardness** of a brush.

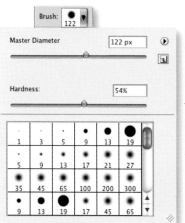

The Brush Presets panel allows for quick selection of a brush preset, along with simple settings such as Diameter and Hardness.

Keyboard Resizing: You can change the Diameter of the active brush via your keyboard by pressing the bracket keys **]** and **[**. You can also change the **Hardness** setting of your brush by holding the **Shift** key while using the bracket keys mentioned above. When using these keyboard commands, the brush will change in preset amounts (0, 25, 50, 75 and 100 for Hardness for example). I use these keyboard shortcuts primarily out of habit since they've been available for many years. I like being able to type the Hardness shortcut four times to be able to get to the softest or hardest setting available.

Drag-Resizing: I really enjoy this new method the most (used as described on the previous page) because I can see a real-time preview of the effect of the **Hardness** setting. This makes it much easier to match the edge quality of an object around which I want to paint. This is my go-to method for quickly changing brush settings and has largely replaced the keyboard commands mentioned earlier.

Smoother Tablet Tracking: If you use a graphics tablet, such as those made by Wacom, you'll be happy to find that your brush cursor will more accurately reflect the movement of the pen. Overall, the pen to screen interaction will feel more fluid and will produce fewer transition artifacts. It's not the easiest thing to describe in text and pictures. You have to get some hands-on experience to really get a sense of what I'm talking about. You might find that your hand simply feels more connected to your brush without any clumsy computer interpretation fouling things up.

Retouching Tools

Photoshop's retouching tools got quite a bit of attention in the CS4 upgrade. The changes make working with the tools much more enjoyable and their functionality has greatly improved.

Clone & Heal Preview Cursors

When cloning, it's now much easier to line up the clone source and destination areas. When you **Option-click** (Mac), or **Alt-click** (Win) on

an area with the **Clone** or **Healing Brush** tools, your cursor will be filled with a preview of the area from which you are cloning. When you move your mouse over the area that needs to be retouched, this preview removes all the guesswork that was involved in previous versions. If you do not like the preview, feel free to turn off both the

You can access the Clone Source panel shown above by choosing Window>Clone Source or by clicking the Clone Source icon that's found in the Options bar when an associated retouching tool is active.

Show Overlay and the **Clipped** checkboxes in the **Clone Source** panel (which can be accessed by clicking the **Clone Source** icon—which looks like a rubber stamp—in the **Options** bar).

This in-brush-preview capability was borrowed from Photoshop's **Vanishing Point**, and I'm honestly surprised it's taken this long it make its way into the **Clone Source** panel.

On occasion, this simple preview-in-a-brush isn't enough to perfectly align two areas. Sure you can try to eyeball it by approximating where an element should be placed, but if you need more precision, you might want to consider changing the **Mode** pop-up menu in the **Clone Source** panel

The blending mode pop-up menu that's found in the Clone Source panel.

(not to be confused with the **Mode** pop-up menu that's found in the Options bar at the top of your screen). **Normal** mode will show the content you're about to apply without attempting to make it blend into the underlying image. **Darken** mode will only show the areas of the source image that are darker than the underlying image, while **Lighten** mode will only show the areas that are brighter than the underlying image. **Difference** mode will display identical areas as solid black while areas that do not match will show as various colors. The best choice will vary depending on how different the source is from the area you are attempting to retouch.

Examples of different blending modes in use (cloning from area to the right), counter clockwise from upper left: Normal, Darken, Lighten, Difference.

This unretouched image contains a horizontal line that should be removed.

Result of using Difference mode to show where two areas are misaligned

The two areas are now in alignment, so they appear as solid black with the exception of the content that is being removed.

Result of removing a portion of the horizontal line while the two areas are in alignment.

Left: Original image.

Below Left: Desaturated with Vibrance checkbox turned off.

Below Right: Desaturated with Vibrance checkbox turned on.

Vibrant Sponge

A **Vibrance** checkbox has been added to the **Sponge** tool. You'll find the **Sponge** tool in the same

slot as the **Dodge** and **Burn** tools in the Tool bar. When the **Vibrance** checkbox is turned off, the **Sponge** tool will act like it did in previous versions of Photoshop, increasing or decreasing the saturation of the area over which you are painting, depending on the setting you've chosen from the **Mode** pop-up menu in the **Options** bar (**Saturate** or **Desaturate**).

The **Vibrance** checkbox is inspired by (but not exactly the same as) the **Vibrance** slider that's found in Adobe Camera Raw and in the new **Vibrance** adjustment in Photoshop CS4. When desaturating an image, turning **Vibrance** on will cause the **Sponge** tool to concentrate on the colors in your image that are less vivid, while leaving overly saturated colors largely unchanged. This can really help to make the colorful areas stand out by de-emphasizing the mellow colors that might draw your eye away from the main subject of your image.

When saturating an image with the **Sponge** tool, the **Vibrance** option can give unexpected results, especially as compared to the way it behaves in Camera Raw or as an Adjustment Layer. Increasing saturation with the **Vibrance** option turned on will cause the image to become brighter as well as more saturated, but it does not cause the tool to concentrate on mellow colors. In fact, turning on the **Vibrance** checkbox often causes a larger change to the already saturated colors in the image, which is the opposite of what the **Vibrance** slider does in other areas of Photoshop. I find that increasing saturation with the **Vibrance** checkbox turned off is often a more effective method for preventing saturated colors from becoming overly saturated.

Original image.

Saturation increased with Vibrance checkbox turned on.

Saturation increased with Vibrance checkbox turned off.

Saturation decreased with Vibrance checkbox turned on.

Saturation decreased with Vibrance checkbox turned off.

Updated Dodge & Burn Tools

Historically, the **Dodge** and **Burn** tools have had a reputation for being somewhat crude and un-refined, often turning wine into water. Darken-ing an image with the **Burn** tool would too easily increase the saturation of the image so much that skin tones would appear to be sunburned and other objects would simply look out of place and unnatural. Lightening an image with the **Dodge** tool would usually produce gray areas that ap-peared artificial, so most people (at least those who insisted on professional-looking results) ended up ignoring these tools altogether.

In Photoshop CS4, Adobe add-ed a **Protect Tones** checkbox in the **Options** bar for both the **Dodge** and **Burn** tools. This checkbox is designed to prevent color shifts when brightening or darkening an image. I find that the this new option makes the **Burn** tool much more effective when used on skin tones and other objects. The **Dodge** tool seems to be a bit more hit and miss with its results—occasional-ly producing over-saturated colors—but at times it seems to work just fine.

*Left: Original image.
Lower Left: Neck and shoulders darkened using the Burn tool with the Protect Tones checkbox turned off.
Lower Right: Image darkened with the Protect Tones checkbox turned on.
Bottom: Enlarged view.*

In the past I've always suggested staying away from the **Dodge** and **Burn** tools, but now I'd be willing to try them on any job. I'd still be on my guard for unnatural-looking results, but your chances of getting what you want from these tools has been greatly increased.

Notes Tool

In the previous version of Photoshop, you had two options for annotating your file. You could use the **Audio Annotation** tool to speak into your computer's microphone, or you could use the **Notes** tool to type little messages, both of which would stay with the file and were identified by little icons placed on top of your image.

In an attempt to update the interface and clean up some of the underlying code, Adobe did away with the **Audio Annotations** tool, but gave the **Notes** tool a whole lot more functionality.

The revamped **Note** tool (notice it dropped the "s") moved higher up in the **Tool** bar and is found in the same slot as the **Eyedropper** tool. Just click and hold on the **Eyedropper** tool to access the icon. Clicking within an image while the **Note** tool is active will deposit a note icon onto the image and make the **Notes** panel visible. If you create more than one note, the active note icon will feature lines and a pencil icon, while other notes will look plain. Clicking on a plain note will make it active. You can cycle through the notes in a document using the left and right arrow icons that are found at the bottom of the **Notes** panel. Clicking the **Trash** icon at the bottom of the **Notes** panel will delete the active note. You can delete all the notes by **Control**-clicking (Mac),

You can access the Notes panel via the Window menu, or by clicking the Notes icon in the Options bar when the Note tool is active.

or **Right**-clicking (Win) on any of the note icons and choosing **Delete All Notes** from the pop-up menu that appears.

At any time you can change the color of the icon used for a note, indicate the author of the note, clear all the notes from your document, or open the **Notes** panel via choices that are found in the **Options** bar near the top of your screen.

This Options bar will appear near the top of your screen when the Note tool is active.

You also have the option of hiding the note icons from view by choosing **View>Show>Notes**. When the note icons are hidden, you can still review their content in the **Notes** panel. This is nice when you have created a bunch of notes but still need to work on your document, and don't want the icons to clutter up your screen. In previous versions you could toggle **View>Extras** to hide the icons, but other important items (such as selection edges and ruler guides) would disappear as well. This is a much better arrangement.

Once you've added notes to an image, you can save the document in any of the following file formats: Photoshop (psd), Large Document Format (psb), Photoshop PDF or TIFF. When saving the file, just make sure the **Notes** checkbox is turned on in the **Save As** dialog box.

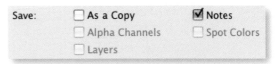

Be sure to turn on the Notes checkbox when saving a document if you want them included in the file.

As with previous versions, you can save your image in PDF format and read the notes from within Adobe Acrobat. That's a great way to send a client comments since Adobe Acrobat Reader is a free download from Adobe.com. You'll have to use the full version of Adobe Acrobat if you want to be able to add or edit notes after it's been saved to PDF.

You have two methods for getting PDF notes back into your original, layered Photoshop file: **1)** Use the new **Preserve Photoshop Editing Capabilities** checkbox in the **Save Adobe PDF** dialog box (which appears after you choose the Photoshop PDF file format in the **File>Save As** dialog box) and then simply re-open the PDF file in Photoshop when you want to view edited notes. The checkbox mentioned above is new to Photoshop CS4 and will make the PDF file incompatible with previous versions of Photoshop. **2)** If you need to be able to open the PDF file in previous versions of Photoshop, turn off the **Preserve Photoshop Editing Capabilities** checkbox when saving the file. If you make changes or add notes in Acrobat, you can re-import them into the original Photoshop file via the **File>Import>Notes** command. By feeding that command an updated PDF file, any notes that were added will be added to the Photoshop file.

These options are available in the PDF Options dialog box which appears when saving a PDF file from Photoshop.

Rotate View Tool

You can now view your images at odd angles without modifying the contents of the document. This is useful when working with a graphics tablet where you might find it more comfortable to hold the tablet at an angle on your lap or desktop. Rotating the image to the same angle as the tablet can make for a more enjoyable experience. To access the new **Rotate View** tool, click and hold on the **Hand** tool and choose it from the pop-up menu that appears.

To rotate your image, simply click and drag within the image window (hold **Shift** to constrain the rotation to 15° increments). As you drag, Photoshop will show a compass overlay with a red arrow that points to whatever was originally the top of your document (an indication

The compass overlay appears when rotating an image.

of 'true north,' so to speak). You can also rotate an image by entering a number in the **Rotation Angle** field or by dragging within the rotation circle that appears in the **Options** bar. If you have more than one image open at a time, turning on the **Rotate All Windows** checkbox in the **Options** bar will cause all open documents to be rotated to the same angle.

The Options bar for the Rotate View tool.

Setting the **Rotation Angle** to zero or clicking the **Reset View** button in the **Options** bar will return you to a non-rotated view of the active document. The view rotation setting is not saved with your image, so the next time you open the file, it will always reset the **Rotation Angle** to zero. Working with a rotated image is only possible because most of the processing involved is being off-loaded to the GPU chip on your graphics card. Be forewarned, you may find this feature to be unavailable when using a computer that does not have an up-to-date video card.

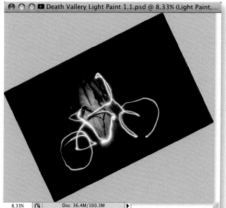

An image that's been rotated using the Rotate View tool.

Navigation Methods

A considerable number of changes have been made to the way you navigate an image. These new features relate to the **Hand** and **Zoom** tools as well as many menu items. Here's what you can look forward to:

Bird's Eye View

Adobe has added a fantastic new way to quickly navigate a document. When you're viewing an image at a magnification that is too great to be able to see the entire image, you can hold the **H** key and press (and hold) the mouse button to temporarily zoom out so you can see the entire image. When you're in this fit-in-window view, a rectangle will indicate the area of the image you were previously viewing. Dragging the rectangle to a new location and releasing the mouse button will cause you to be zoomed into the new location. I think this feature is absolutely awesome and I find myself using it about every three seconds.

Pan and Zoom Preferences

There are three new options related to panning and zooming that are found in the **General** section of Photoshop's **Preferences** dialog box, which is accessed via the **Photoshop** menu (Mac), or **Edit** menu (Win). Here's what's new:

☑ Animated Zoom
☑ Zoom Resizes Windows
☐ Zoom with Scroll Wheel
☐ Zoom Clicked Point to Center
☑ Enable Flick Panning

Animated Zoom: This option (which is on by default) causes changes of magnification to be animated as if you were smoothly changing the magnification using a zoom lens on a camera (as opposed to how it was in previous versions where zooming caused abrupt changes between magnifications), and is very easy on the eyes.

Animated Zoom, along with most other features that depend on the GPU of your video card, will not work on all machines. Older video cards just don't have the power needed for these processing-hungry features. For them to work properly, you need an up-to-date video card.

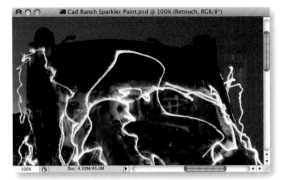

Viewing a small portion of an image.

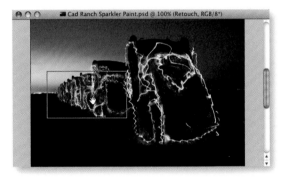

Clicking the mouse button while holding the H key invokes Bird's Eye View. The rectangle initially indicates the area you were previously viewing. Dragging your mouse allows you to quickly navigate to a different area of the image.

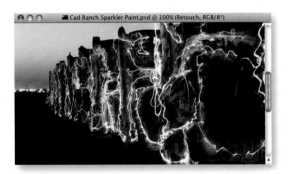

Result of releasing the mouse button in the position shown from Bird's Eye View.

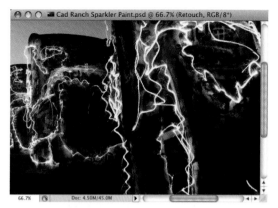

View before clicking with the Zoom tool in the lower right corner of the image.

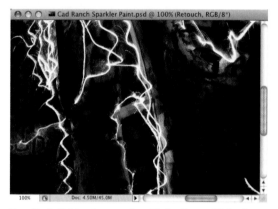

Result of clicking to zoom in with the Zoom Clicked Point to Center checkbox turned off.

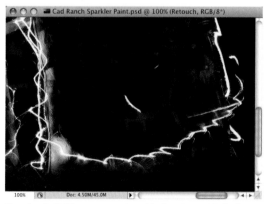

Result of clicking to zoom in with the Zoom Clicked Point to Center checkbox turned on.

Zoom Clicked Point to Center: With this option turned on, any area you click on with the **Zoom** tool will become centered in the document window. I prefer to leave this option turned off because I like how previous versions worked where the clicked area remains under my mouse button, but you may enjoy using this option when combined with the new **Continuous Zooming** feature (which we'll talk about later in this chapter).

Enable Flick Panning: This option will cause any scrolling to briefly continue if you release the mouse button while it is still in motion. This is similar to taking a pool cue and gently tapping a ball on a pool table—after tapping it, the ball would continue to move across the table due to the momentum you created. When this option is enabled, and the panning is in the momentum stage, you can immediately stop the movement by clicking your mouse anywhere on the image, getting the same effect as placing your hand on that moving pool ball.

Pan and Zoom Options

The **Preferences** dialog box is not the only place where you'll find pan and zoom controls. The following options are scattered throughout Photoshop's interface:

Continuous Zooming: You can now press and hold the mouse button when using the **Zoom** tool to continuously zoom into an image. Just release the mouse button when you get to the magnification you desire. The same goes for the reverse, when you add the **Option** key (Mac), or **Alt** key (Win), to zoom out again.

Pixel Grid: If you turn on the **View>Show>Pixel Grid** option, and view your image at a magnification above 600%, Photoshop will display a rectangle around each individual pixel that makes up your image.

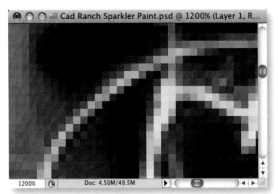

1200% view shown with the Pixel Grid turned off.

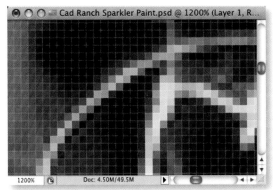

Turning the Pixel Grid on causes the pixels to be outlined in gray when the image is viewed at high magnifications.

Zoom Shortcuts: The new keyboard shortcuts for the **View>Actual Pixels** command—which zooms your document to 100% view—are **Command-1** (Mac), or **Ctrl-1** (Win). This was done to be consistent with keyboard shortcuts that are found in Adobe InDesign and Adobe Illustrator. The old keyboard shortcuts of **Option-Command-0** (Mac) and **Alt-Ctrl-0** (Win) also still work (that's a Zero, not an "Oh" by the way).

Fill Screen Button: The **Zoom** tool and **Hand** tool now feature a **Fill Screen** button in the **Options** bar that will change the magnification of your image so that it fills your entire screen. Unlike the **Fit Screen** button which would ensure that you can see the entire contents of an image, the **Fill Screen** button will usually cut off some of your image because the aspect ratio of your screen is usually different from that of your image.

Fit Screen displays the full image at the largest size possible for your screen size.

Fill Screen cuts off some of the image if it doesn't match the aspect ratio of your screen.

Gesture Support

Sorry, Windows people, you might want to skip this section so you don't feel left out. Right now gesture support is only available for certain Mac models. MacBook owners read on.

You can now navigate your documents using two fingers on the trackpad of a MacBook or MacBook Pro laptop. The following gestures will navigate your images in Photoshop CS4:

Zoom: To increase the magnification of the image, touch your thumb and forefinger together, place them on the trackpad and then spread your fingers apart. To reduce the magnification of your image, start with two fingers spaced apart widely and pinch them together.

Scroll: Place two fingers close together on the trackpad and drag them in any direction. You'll end up scrolling your document in the direction you drag. If nothing happens, make sure you're in a view that does not display the entire image.

Rotate View: Place two outstretched fingers on the trackpad and twist them as if you are spinning an object on a table.

Misc. Changes

Okay, we've explored all the major changes to the tools in Photoshop, now it's time to look at what else might be lurking in the shadowy corners of Photoshop CS4.

Spring-Loaded Keyboard Shortcuts

Adobe has changed the way the tool keyboard shortcuts work. If you press and release the shortcut key, you will switch to the tool and stay in that tool after the mouse is released. If, on the other hand, you press and hold a keyboard shortcut to access a tool, the tool will only stay active for the amount of time you have that key held down. This might sound like a subtle change, but it can radically change the way you work with tools.

Let's say that you've just made a complex selection using the **Lasso** tool and you suddenly need to use the **Marquee** tool to add to the selection. Press and hold the **M** key and you'll see the **Marquee** tool become active. While still holding the **M** key, you can press **Shift** and drag to add to the active selection (**Shift** always adds to a selection, even when not using the new spring loaded keyboard shortcuts). Upon releasing the **M** key, you'll be back in the **Lasso** tool where you can continue to modify the selection. Let's say you've completed the selection, and you want to paint within it, so you press and hold the **B** key and drag the mouse to paint. Upon releasing the mouse, you continue to modify the active selection with the **Lasso** tool. The concept of spring-loaded keyboard shortcuts has the potential to dramatically increase your efficiency in Photoshop.

Modified Selection Edges

Adobe has made a rather subtle change to the appearance of the "marching ants" that indicate the edge of a selection. The new "ants" are made out of longer dashes with a tiny bit more space between each dash, and they have a slightly different animation effect. You'll have to see it for yourself because a screen shot doesn't really convey what's changed.

Eyedropper Sampling

You'll find a new **Sample** pop-up menu in the **Options** bar for the **Eyedropper** tool. When the menu is set to **All Layers**, the **Eyedropper** tool will work just as it has in previous versions, sampling what your image would look like if the image was flattened into a single layer. When the menu is set to **Current** layer, the **Eyedropper** will ignore all layers except the active one and will also disregard how the active layer might be interacting with the underlying images. This means that if you have a layer with a blending mode set to anything other than Normal, the **Eyedropper** will only see the unblended version of that layer, not what you are seeing on your screen.

The Options bar for the Eyedropper tool.

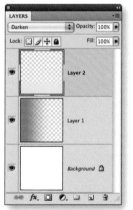

The layers shown above produced the document shown on the right.

Clicking in the lower left corner of the document to the left produced the two colors below: Left=All Layers, Right=Current Layer.

Now that you've officially been introduced to the new features that come with the tools in Photoshop CS4, it's time to go forth and practice, practice, practice. If ever there were a time when it was worth your while to learn new features and shortcuts, now is that time. The new spring-loaded tool switching shortcuts, combined with the drag-resizing features are enough to save you untold hours of needless clicking and mouse-ing, not to mention the divine new pan, zoom, and rotate view options.

I don't think any of us are really conscious of how much time we waste working with tools and getting around in Photoshop (which is probably for the best). My suspicion is that some beady-eyed accountant type at Adobe sat hunched over a calculator and literally figured out how many hours could be saved if the tools were tweaked in such a way that made them more fluid and intuitive. However these changes came to be, we should all be grateful because tooling around in Photoshop just got a whole heck of a lot better.

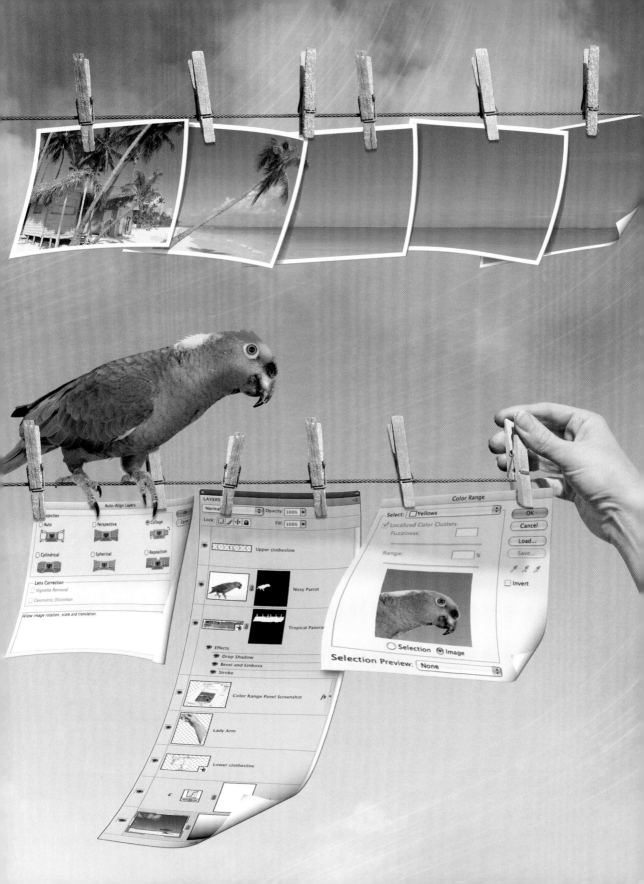

Chapter 6
Layers

A DOBE'S SORCERERS MUST HAVE BURNED the midnight oil as they conjured up the temptations that await you in the ever-evolving world of layers. The most tantalizing offering in the CS4 brew is the dazzling new Content-Aware Scaling feature, which is so wickedly awesome it just might be illegal.

Below is an overview of what we'll be covering in this chapter:

- **Content-Aware Scale:** This new feature allows you to make your images take up more or less space without scaling important content. You have to see it in action to believe it's possible.
- **Auto-Align Layers:** Learn about the new Spherical and Collage alignment methods, as well as the new lens distortion correction.
- **Auto-Blend Layers:** You can now combine multiple images that have limited depth of field to produce a result where everything is in focus.
- **Photomerge:** Learn how to take full advantage of panorama stitching and image stacking.
- **Smart Objects:** See how to work with linked masks and perform perspective transformations, while being fully aware of the pitfalls.
- **Masks Panel:** When you mask a layer to limit where it affects your image, you now have much more versatility with this new panel including a Layer Mask density control.
- **Misc. Changes:** Learn about a few new scripts and other small changes waiting for you in Photoshop CS4.

Where's My Stuff?

Thankfully, Adobe must have decided to give us all a break when it came to messing with the comfortable and familiar layers environment from CS3. Other than replacing the word palette with panel—it's now and forever called a Layers *panel*—there's very little missing from CS3 when it comes to layers. Here's what to look out for when transitioning to the newest version:

- **Layer>Change Layer Content:** This command has gone missing in Photoshop CS4 and no replacement was introduced.
- **Manual Panorama Stitching:** This is another casualty you'll have to deal with when upgrading to Photoshop CS4. To be honest, I haven't used this feature in years because the auto-alignment algorithms are so good, I simply haven't needed it and I stitch hundreds of panoramas each year.

Content-Aware Scale

This new feature feels like the coolest thing on earth and is sure to be a crowd pleaser in any Photoshop demo. Choosing **Edit>Content-Aware Scale** will cause Photoshop to display corner and side handles around the active layer (if the Background is active, choose **Select>All** before trying this feature). Moving any of the handles will scale your image while attempting to leave the important objects within the image untouched. It works like magic with images that have either plain backgrounds or obvious contrast between the important elements and their surroundings. However, even with complex images where the distinction isn't so obvious, there are easy-to-use options that will help you tell Photoshop which elements need protecting.

In the example below, Photoshop correctly determined that the gas station and sign were the important elements of the image and largely left them untouched. Space was added by applying vertical scaling to the smooth sky and by extending the sign post on the right of the image. The results are not perfect; the top left edge of the building was distorted in the process.

Amount

You can also combine traditional scaling with the new **Content-Aware Scale** feature by adjusting the **Amount** setting that's found in the Options bar. For instance, setting the **Amount** to 80% will use a combination of 80% content-aware scaling along with 20% normal scaling. An amount of 0% would cause the **Content-Aware Scale** feature to work just like **Edit>Free Transform**, distorting the shape of all objects within the scene in the process.

The **Content-Aware Scale** feature is by no means perfect. Depending on what's in your image, it's not unusual for it to distort important elements in the scene while leaving unimportant areas unaffected. Let's look at two options that help control the scaling effect.

Original image before scaling has been applied.

Content-Aware Scale with Amount setting of 100%.

Content-Aware Scale with Amount setting of 0%.

Content-Aware Scale with Amount setting of 50%.

Protect Skin Tones

Toggling the **Protect Skin Tones** icon will cause the **Content-Aware Scale** command to protect any areas that resemble skin tones. This is a great feature for those times when a person is the subject of your photograph, but their surroundings are busy enough to fool the **Content-Aware Scale** feature into thinking the background is more important than the subject. If this option is not successful in fixing the problem, you'll have to create a protection mask.

Protection Mask

The **Protect** pop-up menu found in the Options bar allows you to use an Alpha Channel to define the areas that are important in an image and therefore which areas should not be distorted during scaling (similar to how the Freeze Mask tool works in the Liquify filter). To create an Alpha Channel, select the areas you want to preserve using any of Photoshop's selection tools, and choose **Select>Save Selection**. Then, when using the **Content-Aware Scale** feature, choose the name of the Alpha Channel you just created from the **Protect** pop-up menu in the Options bar.

On occasion you'll run into an image where it seems impossible to separate it into areas that should be protected and areas that should be scaled—everything in the image is of some importance. When that's the case, you might want to consider creating a complex mask that includes shades of gray.

When painting with shades of gray, I think of my choices as follows: 0% black (white really) will receive 0% scaling, areas that are 50% gray will be allowed to have up to 50% scaling, while areas that are 100% black will be allowed to be scaled up to 100%. This means that you can start by selecting the areas that should not receive any scaling, save the selection and then go paint on the resulting Alpha Channel with shades of gray to influence how other areas will be treated. The concept of using shades of gray can give you much more influence over how your image is scaled, but you might find it to be beyond your means if you're not overly comfortable with channels and masks.

The Options bar near the top of your screen determines how the Content-Aware Scale command affects your image.

Original image before scaling has been applied.

Scaled with Edit>Free Transform.

Content-Aware Scale without skin protection.

Content-Aware Scale using skin protection.

Original image before scaling has been applied.

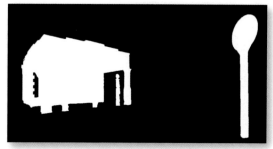

Mask used when scaling the image below.

Result of scaling without a protection mask. The sign-post is being unevenly scaled, becoming skinnier at the bottom as the image is scaled horizontally. A small portion of the right column on the building is also becoming slightly distorted.

Result of scaling using the mask shown above. Notice that the width of the sign post is now consistent and there is no distortion in the columns of the building.

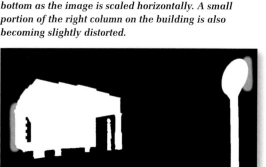

Mask used when scaling the image at right.

Adding some gray to the edge of the building and sign prevented those areas from being scaled so much.

Original image before scaling has been applied.

Result of scaling the image to 60% of its original width with no protection being applied. This results in the fenders of the truck being distorted too much.

Protection mask used when scaling the image at right.

Painting on a mask with solid white causes areas to be protected 100% which causes all the distortion to be applied to the grill of the truck.

Protection mask used when scaling the image at right.

Using white on the edges of the fenders helps to retain their shape, while using a shade of gray in the center of the fender allows those areas to be scaled slightly while still concentrating the scaling onto the grill of the truck.

When you're done scaling the image, either click the **Commit** icon (which looks like a check mark) in the Options bar, press **Return** (Mac), or **Enter** (Win), or double-click within the scaling rectangle.

This new method of scaling is not without its flaws and often requires some retouching afterwards to fix elements that became too distorted as a result of the scaling. With that said, it more than makes up for its inadequacies. Trying to do the same thing in previous versions of Photoshop often involved hours of selecting and scaling and blending multiple layers and retouching, and was not, by any means, an enjoyable process.

Auto-Align Layers

The **Auto-Align Layers** command (which is found under the **Edit** menu) is not new to Photoshop CS4, but there have been a few important additions made. Before we get into the new goodies, let's step back and take a look at what the command is intended to accomplish.

Auto-Align Layers is designed to line up identical content that is found in more than one layer. This can be useful for two purposes: **1)** stitching panoramas that were shot by taking multiple photographs with overlapping content, **2)** aligning multiple shots that contain very similar content such as a series of exposures that vary in brightness, focus point, or contain the same composition but vary in some way (like multiple takes of a group where some people have their eyes closed and you need to composite them into the photo where everyone else's eyes are open).

To align multiple layers, select the layers within the **Layers** panel, choose **Edit>Auto-Align Layers** and then choose between the options you are presented with. Adobe didn't remove any of the options that were available in previous versions, but they did make a few important additions including two new methods for aligning images.

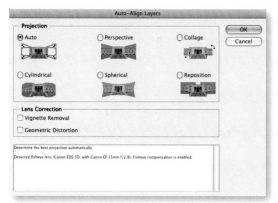

Choosing Edit>Auto-Align Layers will produce the dialog box shown above.

Spherical

The new **Spherical** option is the opposite of the **Cylindrical** option from the previous version. The **Cylindrical** choice bends the edges of your image so that they curve outwards and was often the best method for stitching most panoramas in Photoshop CS3. The new **Spherical** option will bend the edge of images so that they curve inwards. This will produce quite a different look than the **Cylindrical** option and is better at stitching panoramas that extend both horizontally and vertically. It can even stitch a full 360° panorama.

Collage

This new option is limited to scaling, rotating and repositioning layers and is not usually the best choice for traditional stitched panoramas. What it does allow for is the look of a stack of traditional printed photographs that have been reoriented to align as best as can be. I often add **Drop Shadow** and **Stroke** Layer Styles to each layer after applying this alignment choice to make the result resemble a stack of Polaroid® photos.

Fisheye Correction

There's a hidden feature built into the **Auto** setting in the **Auto-Align Layers** dialog box. When that setting is used, Photoshop is able to correct for the distortion caused by using certain fisheye lenses. For this to work, the images you use must contain metadata about the lens that was used. That means you should use files that were created directly from your digital camera, and that scanning a negative or slide is not an option. Photoshop will indicate if it's found the necessary information by displaying the following message near the bottom of the **Auto-Align Layers** dialog box: Fisheye compensation is enabled.

FISHEYE LENSES SUPPORTED		
Brand	**Mount**	**Focal Length**
Canon	Canon	15mm
Sigma	Canon or Nikon	15mm
Sigma	Canon or Nikon	4.5mm
Sigma	Nikon	8mm
Nikon	Nikon	16mm

The ten photographs shown below were combined using the new Collage setting in the Photomerge dialog box (with the Blend Images Together checkbox turned off) to produce the image shown at the right. Stroke, Drop Shadow and Bevel & Emboss Layer Styles were added to each layer in the image to produce the final image that is shown above.

Using the Auto-Align command on the Auto setting with the Blend Images Together option, these three fisheye images combined to create the above image.

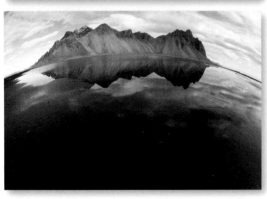

Photoshop was unable to stitch the two images shown above. Including an intermediate third image would have possibly allowed for success, but darn it, those are the only two shots I have available.

This new feature opens up a new world for people who stitch panoramas. As with any stitching method, you'll still need a good amount of overlap between images. Also, be careful of elements that are very close to the lens—that's when you'll need to take additional shots and have even more overlap than you might be used to.

Vignette Removal

The new **Vignette Removal** option will attempt to compensate for the darkened edges that you might encounter when shooting with certain wide angle lenses. Culprit lenses just can't deliver enough light to the edge of your images and will produce a darker edge that's known as vignetting. Stitching images like that in previous versions of Photoshop would often produce telltale uneven skies, which this new feature should help avoid.

Geometric Distortion

This new option is designed to compensate for distortion caused by extreme wide angle and telephoto lenses. Wide angle lenses have a tendency to cause vertical lines to bow outward when they appear near the edge of a scene (a fisheye lens being the widest angle lens you can get makes this effect overly obvious). Telephoto lenses often suffer from the opposite effect where vertical lines can appear bent inward when they are near the edge of the frame.

The combination of the new **Vignette Removal** and **Geometric Distortion** options means that Photoshop CS4 should be able to stitch a wider variety of images and produce smoother results than previous versions were capable of.

Auto-Blend Layers

The **Auto-Blend Layers** command (which is found under the **Edit** menu) has been expanded from an option-less menu command to a dialog box full of options in Photoshop CS4. This command works hand-in-hand with the **Auto-Align Layers** command. The first is used to align multiple images and the second is used to turn the result into a seamless image.

In previous versions, the **Auto-Blend Layers** command performed two tasks: **1)** masking each layer so you could not see an obvious edge to each image, and **2)** adjusting each layer to ensure that the brightness and color matched across the range of photographs. In Photoshop CS4, those functions have been separated and additional options have been made available.

Blend Method

There are now two ways that the **Auto-Blend Layers** command can analyze a set of layers. With both methods, you must first select multiple layers in the **Layers** panel and then choose **Edit>Auto-Blend Layers**. When you do this, Photoshop will check to see how much overlap there is between the layers and it will automatically choose between the two **Blend Methods**—opting for **Panorama** if there is a small overlap between images, or **Stack Images** if there is a huge overlap. Here's what the two methods are designed to tackle:

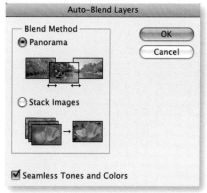

Choosing Edit>Auto-Blend Layers will produce the dialog box shown here.

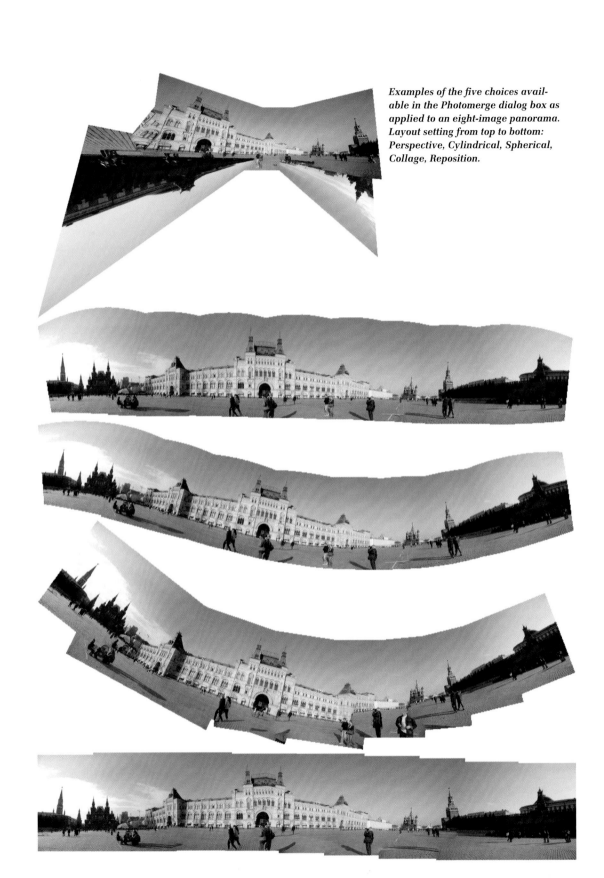

Examples of the five choices available in the Photomerge dialog box as applied to an eight-image panorama. Layout setting from top to bottom: Perspective, Cylindrical, Spherical, Collage, Reposition.

Examples of the five choices available in the Photomerge dialog box as applied to a fifteen-image panorama. Layout setting from top to bottom: Perspective, Cylindrical, Spherical, Collage, Reposition.

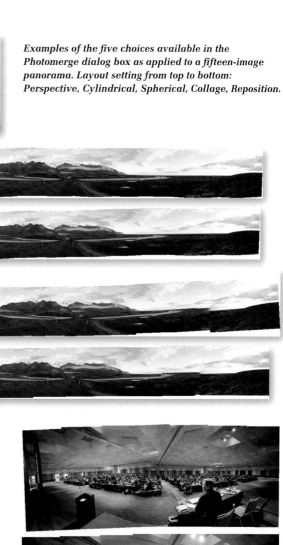

Examples of the five choices available in the Photomerge dialog box as applied to a five-image panorama. Layout setting from top to bottom, left to right: Perspective, Cylindrical, Spherical, Collage, Reposition.

Panorama

This option will attempt to create a seamless panorama by adding **Layer Masks** to each layer and filling areas of the masks with black to hide portions of each layer. This option alone is not usually good enough to produce a finished panorama because it doesn't do anything to make sure the brightness or color is consistent between the images.

Auto-Blend Layers produces Layer Masks that attempt to create a seamless panorama.

Stack Images

This new feature compares the selected layers and masks them in an attempt to keep the highest contrast areas of each layer. Contrast is usually lower in areas that are either out of focus or not properly exposed. You can use this feature to blend exposures or expand the depth of field.

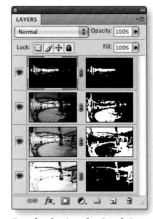

Result of using the Stack Images setting.

Result of Auto-Aligning three fisheye images.

Result of applying the Auto-Blend command.

Moving the layers allows you to better see the distortion caused by aligning the layers.

The Auto-Blend command removed the seams between the image making them fit together like puzzle pieces.

Result of applying the Stack Images option with Seamless Tones and Colors turned off.

Result of applying the Stack Images option with Seamless Tones and Colors turned on.

The same exposures combined using Merge to HDR.

The shots that where combined in the example above.

Blending Exposures: Combining multiple exposures that vary in brightness in an attempt to capture the full brightness range of a scene. This is the same concept as High Dynamic Range (HDR) photography, but offers far less control over the process. The resulting images are often lacking in highlight detail compared to a true HDR image.

Expanded Depth of Field: Used when combining multiple images that have different focus points to expand the depth of field of an image. When a lens delivers a limited depth of field (such as with most macro lenses), only a small portion of the image will be in focus. Taking multiple shots with different focus points will allow you to capture detail in the entire range of the image. Using the **Auto-Blend Layers** command will keep the highest contrast areas of each layer, which usually represents the areas that are in sharp focus. It's very important that the layers be in close alignment, which you can accomplish by either shooting on a sturdy tripod, or by first applying the **Auto-Align Layers** command.

I often find that the **Auto-Align Layers** command is incapable of properly aligning images that contain different focus points. When that's the case, I'll stack the layers manually by temporarily changing the **Blending Mode** pop-up menu at the top of the **Layers** panel to Difference and adjusting the position of the layers until the result looks as close to solid black as possible.

Neither of the Blend Methods are sufficient to produce a seamless image. To produce a truly acceptable result, you'll need to combine those methods with the **Seamless Tones and Colors** checkbox.

Seamless Tones and Colors

This feature will take the results produced by the **Panorama** or **Stack Images** feature and compare the brightness and color of each layer in the resulting layer stack. It will then make adjustments to each layer in an attempt to create a truly seamless image. The only time I don't have this checkbox turned on is when I want to have obvious differences between the layers that make up a panorama, as in the iguana example shown earlier in this chapter.

Result of Auto-Blending Layer on the two images shown below with Seamless Tones and Colors turned off.

Result of Auto-Blending Layer on the two images shown below with Seamless Tones and Colors turned on.

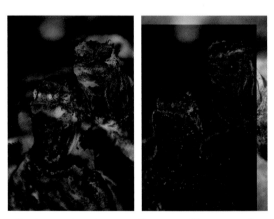

The two images used to create the results shown above. Additional images would be needed in order to produce the full depth of field between these two iguanas because the region between them is not in focus in either shot.

Aligning two images manually using Difference mode. Left: Not aligned. Right: Aligned more closely.

Photomerge

Photomerge is traditionally used as a shortcut when you need to quickly stitch together a seamless panorama. By choosing it in Bridge you take a three step process and turn it into a single step. The **Photomerge** dialog box combines the functionality found in the following three Photoshop features: **1) Load Files into Stack** (which is found under the **File>Scripts** menu), **2) Auto-Align Layers**, and **3) Auto-Blend Layers**. Photomerge is not new to Photoshop CS4, but the changes made to the individual features it utilizes affect how you work with Photomerge.

You start by selecting the images you want to stitch within Bridge. Next, choose **Tools>Photoshop>Photomerge**, choose the **Auto** option and turn on the **Blend Images Together** checkbox (which is the equivalent to the **Seamless Tones and Colors** checkbox in the **Auto-Blend Layers** dialog box) before clicking **OK**. The new

Vignette Removal and **Geometric Distortion Correction** checkboxes are optional. I find that using both **Auto** and **Geometric Distortion Correction** is essential when stitching images shot with a fisheye lens.

With CS4, Adobe has removed the **Interactive Layout** option that was found in previous versions. To be honest, I haven't used that old option since the auto alignment options were introduced in Photoshop CS3. I'm sure some people will miss it, but Adobe has been trying to modernize the code which makes up the underlying structure of Photoshop, and in the process they've removed some rarely used features so they don't have to spend the time needed to modernize them.

You'll need to turn off the **Blend Images Together** checkbox to get the best results when performing exposure blending or expanding depth of field by stacking multiple images. That is best done as a two-step process—use Photomerge to stack the images and then manually run the **Auto-Blend Layers** command to blend the results. Adobe has done it that way because it's not uncommon to need to adjust the positioning and apply manual transformations to ensure that the layers properly align even after the **Auto-Align Layers** command has been utilized.

Choosing Tools>Photoshop>Photomerge from within Bridge will produce the dialog box shown above.

Smart Objects

When Smart Objects were introduced in Photoshop CS2, there were two major flaws in the implementation, both of which have been rectified in Photoshop CS4. Let's first review Smart Objects and how they work before we get into the changes made in CS4.

You can convert one or more layers into a Smart Object by selecting the layers and then choosing **Layer>Smart Objects>Convert to Smart Object**. After doing so, the selected layers will appear as a single layer with a Smart Object badge covering its thumbnail image in the **Layers** panel. You can think of a Smart Object as a protective bubble that contains the original layers.

When working with Smart Objects, you'll be limited to operations that do not change the individual layers contained within the Smart Object. That means you can only do things that can be recorded as settings that are attached to the layer—settings that can easily be changed or removed including:

- **Scale, Rotate and Transformations**
- **Reposition or Change Layer Stacking Order**
- **Layer Styles Added**
- **Change Layer Blending Mode**
- **Add Layer Mask to Hide Areas**

In order to change the contents of the Smart Object, you must double-click its thumbnail in the **Layers** panel to cause the layers to appear as separate documents. After you've made changes, you can choose **File>Save**, which will update the document that contained the Smart Object, and all the changes that were attached to the Smart Object (scaling, rotation, etc.) will reapply.

Now that you have an idea of how Smart Objects work, let's take a look at the two changes they've made in Photoshop CS4.

Smart Objects are marked with a special icon.

Linked Layer Masks

In previous versions of Photoshop, Layer Masks that were attached to Smart Objects could not be linked to the Smart Object. That meant that doing something as simple as moving, scaling or rotating the Smart Object would leave the Layer Mask unchanged. This presented a huge challenge because the content of a Layer Mask almost always relates to the content in a Smart Object, and transforming one while leaving the other untouched will completely mess up the appearance of the document.

That problem has now been solved. When you add a Layer Mask to a Smart Object in Photoshop CS4, the two pieces will automatically be linked as indicated by a chain symbol. When the two are linked, any transformations applied to the layer will affect both the Smart Object and the Layer Mask. This change might seem simple, but it wasn't the easiest thing for Adobe to pull off and there are consequences to contend with.

Clicking in the space between the two thumbnails will toggle the visibility of the chain icon that indicates if the Layer Mask is linked to the layer.

The background on this trailer has been hidden by painting with black in a Layer Mask.

Using the Move tool to reposition the contents of the layer while the Layer Mask is unlinked.

Smart Object Transformations are Parametric

Transformations that are applied to Smart Objects are what's sometimes referred to as being parametric. That's just a fancy word that in Photoshop means you can apply a feature to a layer that doesn't cause it to change permanently. Instead, it applies the change as a simple set of instructions to the layer and those changes can be modified or reset at any time without degrading the quality of the results (just like the **Opacity** setting at the top of the **Layers** panel, which can be changed back to 100% at any time without degrading the contents of a layer).

In fact, you can open a document you created years ago, select the layer that contains a Smart Object, choose **Edit>Free Transform**, and Photoshop will show you the exact scale and rotation settings you applied when you first changed that layer years earlier. Changing the settings back to their defaults would return the Smart Object to the way it looked before any transformations were applied and the quality of the image would not be degraded. It would be as if you decided to cancel the initial transformation before you ever finished applying it. In CS4, adding a linked Layer Mask to the same Smart Object will complicate the matter.

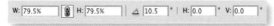

The settings shown in the Options bar when transforming a Smart Object are the parameters of the transformation and can be changed at any time in the future by choosing Edit>Free Transform a second time.

Layer Mask Transformations are Destructive

Transformations applied to Layer Masks are not applied parametrically but will instead permanently change the pixels that make up the mask (this is known as being 'destructive'). That means that if you were to scale a masked Smart Object down until it is only two pixels wide, and then finish the transformation by pressing **Return** (Mac) or **Enter** (Win), Photoshop would treat the two elements of the layer differently: The Smart Object would still contain the full resolution of its original content and appear as being two pixels wide (as a result of the instructions attached

to the Smart Object). The Layer Mask on the other hand won't be so lucky. Its contents will be permanently changed and will end up being two pixels wide with no references to what the mask previously contained.

Mixing Parametric and Destructive Edits

If you were to save and close the document mentioned above, open it a week later and scale the layer back to its original size, the Smart Object would look perfect, as if it had never been scaled before (because the original, full-resolution layers are stored within the Smart Object, and the transformation was just a set of attached instructions), but the Layer Mask would not retain any of its original detail because the earlier transformation was permanent and left only two pixels in the width of the mask, which would, if scaled up, produce an overly blurry mask with no fine detail.

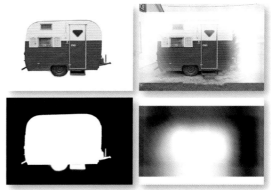

The background on the trailer above is being hidden using the mask shown below. On the right is a version that has been scaled down to a very small size and then re-transformed back to its original size.

Re-Transforming Mixed Edits

It's not uncommon to need to transform a layer more than once. Maybe you rotate the layer to 45° and then an hour later you change your mind and need the layer at 75°. In the past, choosing **Edit>Free Transform** while a Smart Object was active would send you back into the transformation as if you never left the first one. In this example, the transformation rectangle would appear at 45° when you start to re-transform the layer and you'd simply rotate it further until it ended up at 75°.

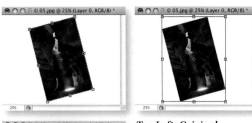

Top Left: Original transformation.
Top Right: Re-transforming a layer containing a linked Layer Mask.
Left: Re-transforming a layer that contains an unlinked Layer Mask.

When you work with a Smart Object that has a linked Layer Mask, things are a little different. If you choose **Edit>Free Transform** on a layer that was previously transformed to a 45° angle, the transformation rectangle will appear perpendicular to the document window, as if the layer contained a photograph that was taken at a 45° angle and then scanned into Photoshop. This takes a little getting used to if you're accustomed to previous versions of Photoshop.

Resetting Previous Transformations

Since Smart Objects made their debut, I've gotten in the habit of being carefree when it comes to transforming them. Why? Because at any time after the original transformation I could again choose **Edit>Free Transform** and the Options bar would display the exact settings I first used to transform the image. I then had the option of changing the settings to their defaults which would return the layer to its original size and rotation, with no loss in quality!

In CS4 it ain't so easy because when you go to re-transform a Smart Object that has a linked Layer Mask attached, the numbers in the Options bar will always display their default settings instead of reflecting the previous transformation you had applied. That's because the transformation applied to the Layer Mask was permanent, making it impossible for Photoshop to keep records on any transformations it might have shared with the linked Smart Object. If you want Photoshop

to keep track of the original transformation settings, click the chain icon that appears between the Layer Mask thumbnail and the Smart Object thumbnail (in the **Layers** panel) to unlink the mask, and click on the Smart Object thumbnail to make it active *before* re-transforming the layer. That will cause the Smart Object to be re-transformed (and maintain its original setting history), while leaving the Layer Mask unchanged.

Warping Unavailable on Linked Smart Objects

After working out all the details mentioned above, Adobe just couldn't come up with an elegant way to allow warping to be applied to Smart Objects that have linked Layer Masks. That's because they would have had to figure out what to do in a situation where you had previously rotated the layer before applying the Warping. With a stand-alone Smart Object it's pretty straightforward because it would simply start the warping rectangle with the same angle at which the layer had been rotated. But a linked Layer Mask complicates that logic because there is no record to indicate if the mask had been previously rotated by the same amount as the Smart Object (maybe the mask was added after the contents of the layer were rotated). If Adobe had followed through with that approach, the warp rectangle would show up rotated on the Smart Object, but straight on the Layer Mask, which wasn't a viable solution. As a consequence, choosing **Edit>Transform>Warp** on a Smart Object linked to a Layer Mask will cause a warning to appear that indicates you must unlink the Layer Mask before you'll be able to warp the Smart Object layer.

This message will appear any time you attempt to apply warping to a Smart Object that has a linked Layer Mask attached.

Whew! What a snarl. Now you know what I meant when I said that Adobe's making the decision to allow you to link a Layer Mask to a Smart Object wasn't exactly a slam dunk.

Distort & Perspective Transformations

In previous versions of Photoshop, when a Smart Object was active, it was not possible to choose **Distort** or **Perspective** from the **Edit>Transform** menu. This limitation has been removed in CS4, which makes Smart Objects much more useful. Let's look at one example of how you can now do things that were not possible in previous versions.

As an author, my publisher needs marketing materials for a project before a book is ever printed. A photograph of the finished book would be ideal but since it's not possible to shoot something that doesn't yet exist, I create photo-realistic faux book covers from scratch in Photoshop (the pages in the book are made by applying the **Noise** and **Motion Blur** filters for example). I've been using the same cover mockup for over a decade and Photoshop CS4 makes updating the faux cover a breeze.

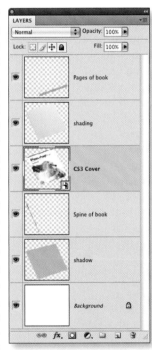

Layers panel view of the document used to create the faux book covers shown to the right.

In previous versions, the process of changing the cover from one version to another was a tedious, manual process. To streamline the update process in Photoshop CS4, I opened an undistorted color design (in its original form used to print the actual book cover), selected all the layers that made up that document and chose **Layer>Smart Objects>Convert to Smart Object**.

I then dragged the newly created Smart Object to my book mock-up file, chose **Edit>Transform>Distort** and adjusted the corner handles of the transformation rectangle until they matched the corners of the existing book cover within the mock-up.

Now, all I have to do to update the faux book cover image is to choose **Layers>Smart Objects>Replace Contents** when the book cover Smart Object layer is active and supply Photoshop with a different undistorted cover design file. Doing so causes Photoshop to update the cover layer and automatically reapply the distortion that makes it match the mock-up image. I haven't even started to think about the cover design that I'll use for the Photoshop CS4 version of the book, but now that the faux cover document is set up, changing it over to my next cover design will take seconds and I can update it at anytime as the design progresses by simply applying the **Replace Contents** command.

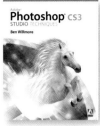

The cover design as used to print the actual book was used to replace the contents of the Smart Object layer.

NOTE

Using Smart Objects
You can find an introduction to Smart Objects and much more detail about their usage in my *Photoshop Studio Techniques* book, which just happens to be the book I originally created the faux book cover for.

Top Left: Book cover created before Smart Objects were available. Top Right: Cover replaced with a Smart Object that has been transformed to the same perspective. Left: Replaced contents with updated cover.

Masks Panel

A mask is something that's added to a layer to control where the layer will be visible or hidden. There are two types of masks available: **Layer Masks** are grayscale images where black causes areas of a layer to become hidden, white causes areas to be visible, and shades of gray cause an area

Choose Window>Masks to open the new Masks panel.

to become translucent. **Vector Masks** on the other hand are based on paths (also known as vectors) that are created with the **Pen** or **Shape** tools. They traditionally have always had razor-sharp edges.

The ability to add masks to layers is not a new feature. In creating Photoshop CS4, Adobe wanted to add some enhancements that relate to Layer Masks and Vector Masks but found that the **Layers** panel (where those types of features historically reside) was already overflowing with icons and controls, so they created the new **Masks** panel. Having a whole separate panel also gave them room to add a few shortcuts for features that existed in previous versions of Photoshop. Here's what you'll find the new Masks panel:

Mask Thumbnail: The thumbnail image that's found in the upper left of the **Masks** panel indicates the type of mask you are currently editing. It will display one of three states:

1) When no mask is active, it will display a thumbnail that shows the contents of the active layer as it appears after the masks have been applied.

2) When a Layer Mask is active it will show you the contents of the mask and will be labeled Pixel Mask (since Layer Masks are made out of pixels).

3) When a Vector Mask is active, the thumbnail will show you a preview of the path that's being used to limit where the active layer is visible.

There is no additional functionality behind these thumbnails—unlike the ones found in the **Layers** panel where you can hold modifier keys and click to perform certain tasks (like disabling the mask).

Add Mask Icons: The two icons that appear in the upper right corner of the **Masks** panel serve multiple functions. The left icon performs tasks relating to Layer Masks, while the right icon is specific to Vector Masks. When either icon includes a **plus sign** (**+**), it's an indication that the active layer does not contain that type of mask. Clicking the icon while it's in that state will add the appropriate type of mask to the active layer. When a mask is present, one of the icons will feature a double border which indicates which mask is active for editing. Clicking on one of the two icons will change which of the two types of masks is active.

Density: This setting determines how far a mask can go in its attempt to hide the contents of a layer. When the **Density** is set to 100%, painting with black in a Layer Mask or adding a path to a vector mask will cause the affected area to become completely hidden from view. Lowering the **Density** to 90% would prevent the contents of the active mask from completely hiding an area and would cause areas that would usually be hidden to appear as 10% opaque. Lowering the **Density** to 30%, would cause the "hidden" areas of the image to appear as 70% opaque.

This new feature is in some ways the opposite of the **Opacity** control that's found at the top of the **Layers** panel. Lowering the **Opacity** affects the visible areas of the layer, causing them to become less opaque and therefore less translucent. Lowering **Density** affects the hidden areas of the layer, causing them to become more visible.

Background removed via a Layer Mask with the Density setting at 100%

The same image as above with the Density setting lowered to 30%

I use the Density slider the most when applying Adjustment Layers. I'll often mask my adjustment to only affect one area of the image and later decide to apply the same adjustment to the rest of the image at a lower opacity. Lowering the **Density** slider gives me the effect I just described.

Black & White adjustment applied using a layer mask to prevent it from applying to the motorhome.

Lowering the Density of the mask to 50% applied 50% of the adjustment to the motorhome while keeping it full strength elsewhere.

Feather: This slider will cause the edge of the active mask to become softer (just like blurring a Layer Mask) without actually changing the contents of the mask.

This new feature can really change the way you think about Vector Masks. In previous versions of Photoshop, the only way you could soften the edge of a Vector Mask was to convert it to a Layer Mask and then apply the **Guassian Blur** filter (thereby destroying the original mask). Now, all you have to do to create a soft edge with a Vector Mask is to adjust the **Feather** slider.

Editing a Layer Mask while the **Feather** setting is turned up can be a dizzying experience. The **Feather** setting will cause all your paint strokes to have soft edges even though you might have been painting with a hard edged brush. If you have the **Feather** setting high enough, your brush strokes might not even show up as black in the mask. If you ever get disoriented from this effect, keep in mind that bringing the Feather setting back to zero will reveal the true contents of the mask.

The rest of the features in the new **Masks** panel are simply shortcuts for things you could have done in previous versions of Photoshop. Here's what you'll find:

Mask viewed with Feather setting at 100 pixels. *The same mask viewed with Feather set to zero.*

Edits made with Feather setting at 100 pixels. *The same mask viewed with Feather set to zero.*

Mask Edge: Clicking this button will cause the **Refine Mask** dialog box to appear. You could access the same dialog box by choosing **Refine Edge** from the **Select** menu in Photoshop CS3.

Color Range: Clicking this button is the same as choosing **Select>Color Range**, which is useful when creating and modifying selections. There have been changes made in the resulting dialog box, but we cover them in Chapter 7.

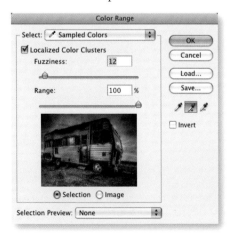

Invert: This button performs the same function as choosing **Image>Adjustments>Invert** which causes black areas in a Layer Mask to turn white while white areas turn black. This effectively reverses the visibility of areas where previously hidden areas will become visible while previously visible areas will become hidden.

All three of the buttons mentioned above will be grayed out when a Vector Mask is active. Now that you know what those buttons do, let's take a look at the icons that appear at the bottom of the **Masks** panel.

Original Layer Mask.   *Inverted mask.*

Image with mask applied.   *Image with inverted mask.*

Load As Selection Icon: Clicking this icon will produce a selection based on the mask that is active. White areas in a Layer Mask will become selected, while black areas will not. This could be done in previous versions of Photoshop by either choosing **Select>Load Selection** and choosing the mask as the source, or by holding **Command** (Mac) or **Ctrl** (Win) and clicking within the Layer Mask thumbnail image for the active layer.

If a selection is already active when you click that icon, the mask-based selection will replace the active one. Holding **Shift** when clicking the icon will add the mask-based selection to the active selection, while holding **Option** (Mac), or **Alt** (Win) will subtract the mask-based selection from the active one. You can also hold both of those keys to only retain the areas of the active selection that overlap the mask-based selection that you are loading.

If you have trouble remembering those keyboard shortcuts, feel free to substitute the appropriate choices that are found in the side menu of the **Masks** panel.

Mask Options...

Add Mask To Selection
Subtract Mask From Selection
Intersect Mask With Selection

Close
Close Tab Group

Apply Mask Icon: This is a shortcut for the **Layer>Layer Mask>Apply** command.  Clicking it will cause hidden areas of a layer to be permanently deleted and the mask will be removed from the layer. Just think of it as merging the mask into the image to permanently apply its changes.

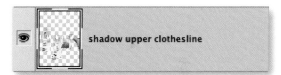

Original image before making the mask permanent.

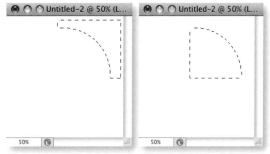

Result of clicking the Apply Mask icon.

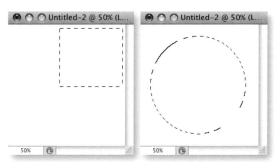

Existing selection. *Masked-based selection.*

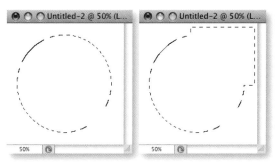

Result of loading the mask-based selection with no keys being held down. *Result of loading the mask-based selection with Shift key held.* *Result of loading the mask-based selection with Option or Alt key held.* *Result of loading the mask-based selection with both keys held.*

Disable Mask Icon: Clicking this icon produces the same result as **Shift**-clicking within the active mask's thumbnail image in the **Layers** panel. It will temporarily disable the mask bringing the full layer into view. A red slash will appear over the icon and an "X" will be overlaid on the mask to give you a visual indication that it has been disabled.

Trash Mask Icon: Clicking this icon is the same as dragging the thumbnail for the active mask to the Trash icon that's found at the bottom of the **Layers** panel. It will remove the mask from the layer and cause any areas that were being hidden by the mask to become visible.

Misc. Changes

Now that you've seen how all the features in the Masks panel work, there's a few other layer-related changes I want to share with you.

New Scripts Added

You'll find two new layer-related additions to the **File>Scripts** menu:

Flatten All Masks: Applying this script has the same effect as if you selected every layer with a Layer or Vector Mask attached and clicked the **Apply Mask** icon that's found in the new **Masks** panel. That effectively makes the effects of the masks permanent. The script will ignore masks that are applied to Adjustment Layers since the only effective method of permanently applying those masks would be to merge the Adjustment Layers into the underlying image.

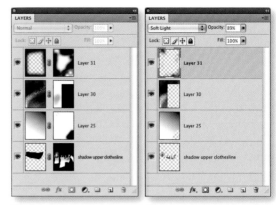

Before applying the new Flatten All Masks script.   *After applying the new Flatten All Masks script.*

I find this script to be especially useful when I need to load a layered Photoshop file into another program that does not understand masks, or when I need to send a layered file to someone and I don't want them to be able to change the effects of the masks.

Flatten All Layer Effects: This script will merge all the Layer Effects (like Drop Shadow or Bevel & Emboss) that are contained in your document into the individual layers to which they are attached. If the layer is a shape or text layer, then the layer will have to be rasterized (turned into pixels) in the process.

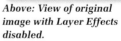

Above: View of original image with Layer Effects disabled.
Above right: Original image with Layer Effects visible.
Right: Result of applying Flatten All Layer Effects script (little or no change).

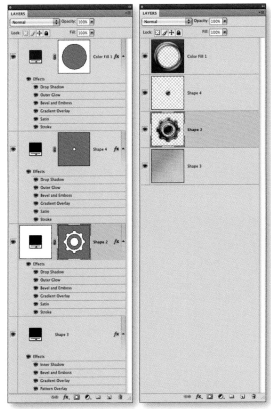

Layers used to produce
original image.

Result of applying Flatten
All Layer Effects script.

The results are the same as placing an empty layer below the layer that has effects applied, clicking on the effects-laden layer and then choosing **Layer>Merge Down**.

I find this script to be useful when I need to load a layered file into a non-Adobe program that would usually ignore Layer Effects.

Stroke Layer Effect Default Changed

Some users will be overjoyed to learn that Adobe has finally changed the default color for Stroke Layer Effects (accessed via the **Layer Effects** pop-up menu at the bottom of the **Layers** panel or via the **Layer>Layer Style** menu) from bright red to black.

I know this seemingly insignificant change doesn't really deserve such a huge headline, but that old red color was like an itch you couldn't scratch. It was like tripping over the same pair of dirty socks in the middle of the living room for ten years and not being able to throw them in the hamper. It was just annoying—I mean, how often do you apply a blazing bright red stroke to your images?—and it's satisfying to be rid of it.

Okay, enough whining about petty issues. We've worked our way through the new layers environment of CS4, and I hope you are as excited about the new features as I am. With the exception of the complication introduced by the new capability to link a Smart Object to a Layer Mask (which I truly think was a worthwhile sacrifice for the enhanced transformation capabilities), there is so much to work with here, all of which should have a enormously positive effect on your workflow and creativity.

The majority of improvements were obviously aimed at more experienced users. Let's face it, working with Smart Objects combined with Layer Masks isn't exactly something you do when you're just starting out. But the truth is that the full-version of Photoshop, while still very serviceable for beginners, has evolved into a highly sophisticated tool designed for professionals, and the upgrades will only continue to be more and more complex.

If you read this chapter and felt overwhelmed by what was covered, spend some time learning more about the basics which you can do by reading my other book, Adobe Photoshop Studio Techniques. And if you're not yet using Layer Masks, I strongly encourage you to take some time and learn everything you can about them. To not use Layer Masks in Photoshop is like buying an expensive new car and only driving it in first gear. You never get that full-throttle, roaring down the highway feeling.

Chapter 7
General Improvements

H ERE YOU'LL FIND A POTPOURRI of features that couldn't find a home in other chapters, many of which have to do with color: how it's used to make a selection, how it's perceived, and how it's managed. There are other goodies as well, in no particular order, so jump in and explore what looks most interesting to you.

Below is an overview of what we'll be covering in this chapter:

- **Color Range:** Learn how the new **Localized Color Clusters** and **Range** control give you more power over color selections, resulting in more accurate and predictable results.
- **Flash Panels:** See how third-party developers can create customized Photoshop panel designs. You'll be introduced to the two samples that Adobe has provided with CS4: the **Kuler** panel (a sophisticated color picker) and the **Connections** panel (which allows you to interface with your online Adobe account).
- **Save for Web & Devices:** See what's new in the redesigned **Save for Web & Devices** dialog box, including enhanced zoom control and metadata options.
- **Color Management:** You can now simulate color blindness, work with linked profiles, and create spot color separations.
- **Misc. Changes:** Find the small and large changes that are lurking in the vast corners of the Photoshop CS4 interface, including the new 64-bit support in Windows and some new options in the **Print** dialog box.

Where's My Stuff?

Here are a few things you should look out for if you've been working with Photoshop CS3:

- **UI Font Setting:** This setting has been moved from the General section to the Interface section of Photoshop's **Preferences** dialog box.
- **Grayscale Toolbar Icon:** The **Use Grayscale Toolbar Icon** has been renamed **Use Grayscale Application Icon** (in keeping with its new location in the Application bar).
- **Legacy Serial Number:** The **Legacy Serial Number** setting is no longer available in Photoshop's Preferences.
- **Pattern Maker & Extract Filters:** Neither of these filters are included with Photoshop CS4, but you can copy them from the Plug-Ins folder in Photoshop CS3 to the equivalent folder in CS4.
- **Pixel Aspect Ratio:** It has been moved from the **Image** menu to the **View** menu.
- **Save For Web & Devices:** So much has changed with this feature that there's an entire Where's My Stuff list in the Save For Web & Devices section of this chapter.

Color Range

If you choose **Select>Color Range**, you'll discover the revised **Color Range** dialog box. This feature has been available in Photoshop for eons, but it's been a bit uncontrollable, often producing undesirable selections. That's changed with the addition of the new **Localized Color Clusters** checkbox and the related **Range** slider (which is only available after you turn on that new checkbox).

The image shown in this dialog box was used in all of the examples shown on these two pages.

Legacy Color Range Behavior

If you ignore the new features by leaving the **Localized Color Clusters checkbox** turned off, the **Color Range** dialog box will act just like it did in previous versions of Photoshop. That's good if you use actions or scripts (because any actions or scripts that utilize the dialog box will still operate as they did without modification), but if you want to take advantage of the new features, you'll need to turn on the **Localized Color Clusters** checkbox. In order to understand the new features, we'll first need to review how **Color Range** has worked in previous versions of Photoshop:

Single Sample Point

To select an area, start by clicking within the active document to indicate the main color you'd like to select. If you're working with a simple image that contains solid areas of color with little variation (like text), a single click might be enough to produce an acceptable selection. After clicking within the image, a preview will

appear at the bottom of the **Color Range** dialog box. In this preview, selected areas appear as white while non-selected areas are black.

Fuzziness

If the area you wish to select varies slightly in color or brightness, you may need adjust the **Fuzziness** slider to control the range of color that will be selected. You can think of this slider as controlling the degree of variation there will be from the color on which you clicked. Using a setting of zero will select only the exact color you've clicked on within the image.

After clicking within the blue area of the example image, the Fuzziness slider was adjusted to the following settings (from left to right): 0, 60, 200.

Working with Multiple Sample Points

If the combination of clicking within your image and adjusting the **Fuzziness** slider is not enough to produce an acceptable selection, you'll need to mess with the eyedropper icons that appear on the right side of the **Color Range** dialog box. The **Eyedropper** tool on the far left is active by default, so clicking within your image determines the main color you plan to select. Clicking a second time with this tool has the effect of canceling out any previous clicks and is useful when you accidentally click on the wrong color within your image.

Clicking on different areas of the image changes the color that Color Range is sampling.

The **Eyedropper** tool that displays a plus sign (**+**) can be used after you've clicked with the main **Eyedropper** tool. Each click with this tool will expand the range of colors being selected. If you click on a yellow area and then click on a blue area with this eyedropper, both colors would be included in your selection. This sounds simple, but is actually a bit more complex. When the new **Localized Color Clusters** checkbox is turned off, clicking on the two colors mentioned above would cause Photoshop to not only select yellow and blue areas, it would also include many colors that would be found in between those two in the color spectrum (think of a rainbow).

If too large of an area is selected, you have two choices to remedy the situation: **1)** reduce the **Fuzziness** setting to narrow the range of colors, or **2)** click within the image while the **Eyedropper** tool with the negative symbol (**-**) is active. Clicking with this tool will allow you to reduce the number of the in-between colors that are included in your selection, but you might find that it will often be too aggressive in reducing the range of colors being selected. Don't get too frustrated because I think you'll find that the new **Localized Color Clusters** feature should make the eyedropper tools much more effective.

Result of clicking in the lower right corner of the image to select the blue areas.   *Result of clicking on the yellow area in the upper left with the Plus Eyedropper tool.*   *Result of clicking in the upper right corner with the Minus Eyedropper tool.*

Each time you enter the **Color Range** dialog box it will start fresh. If you need it to remember where you had clicked with the Eyedroppers when you last used the command, hold the **Option** key (Mac), or **Alt** key (Win) when choosing **Select>Color Range**.

Selection Preview

The preview that is shown at the bottom of the **Color Range** dialog box isn't always the most useful way to preview a selection. By choosing from the **Selection Preview** pop-up menu at the bottom of the dialog box you'll be able to produce a preview within your document window. Here's what you'll find in that menu:

Grayscale: Displays the selection as it would appear in a mask where white represents a selected area, black represents a non-selected area, and shades of gray represent a partially selected area.

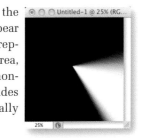

Black Matte: Overlays solid black over areas that are not selected, leaving selected areas untouched. When using this mode, you might want to consider choosing the **Image** option at the bottom of the dialog box so that the mini-preview will display your image instead of a preview.

White Matte: Overlays solid white over areas that are not selected, leaving selected areas untouched.

Quick Mask: Shows the selection as if it were being displayed in Quick Mask mode where non-selected areas are displayed as a semi-transparent colored overlay. The default setting for the overlay is red, but can be changed by double-clicking the **Quick Mask** icon near the bottom of Photoshop's Tool bar.

Invert

Turning on the **Invert** checkbox will cause the state of selected and non-selected areas to be reversed. This can be useful when you want to either select everything but one particular color, or when you need the selection preview to display an overlay on the selected areas instead of the non-selected areas. Just try to remember to turn it back off if you don't need the resulting selection to be inverted.

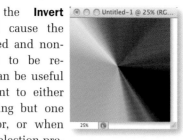

Now that you have an general feeling for how the **Color Range** dialog box works, let's explore the new features that were added in Photoshop CS4.

Localized Color Clusters

Turning on the **Localized Color Clusters** checkbox causes multiple changes to how Color Range creates selections.

True Isolation of Colors

Remember how selecting two colors (like yellow and blue) caused many of the in-between colors to be selected as well? Turning on the **Localized Color Clusters** checkbox will prevent in-between colors from being selected, which really improves the usefulness of the **Color Range** dialog box. With this new functionality, you can easily select yellow, magenta and cyan areas without getting the red, green and blue colors that are found between them in the color spectrum.

Range Setting

When the **Localized Color Clusters** checkbox is turned off, Photoshop will look across every pixel of your image and attempt to find the colors you've sampled with the **Eyedropper** tools in the **Color Range** dialog box. Turning on the **Localized Color Clusters** checkbox not only causes Photoshop to avoid in-between colors, it also causes the new **Range** setting to modify how selections are created. I leave this checkbox turned on for the majority of selections I make, but occasionally I find the new **Range** setting getting in my way, and in those situations I might make a selection with the checkbox turned off.

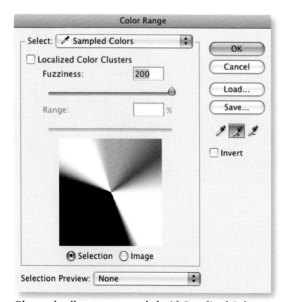

Blue and yellow areas sampled with Localized Color Clusters turned off.

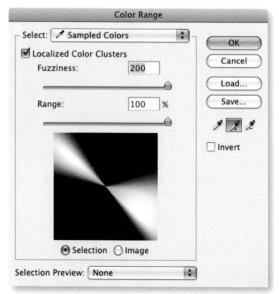

Blue and yellow areas sampled with Localized Color Clusters turned on.

This new setting causes Photoshop to only produce selections within a certain distance of the spot on which you clicked with one of the **Eyedropper** tools. The "analysis area" is circular in shape, with a soft edge, centered on the spot where you clicked. The setting is measured as a percentage of the width or height of the active document (whichever is largest).

The image shown above was used in the example shown below.

Clicking multiple times within your image while the **Plus Eyedropper** tool is active will cause Photoshop to isolate small areas. Clicking and dragging across an area will define a rectangular area to be added to the selection.

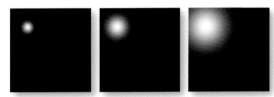

Range settings from left to right: 10%, 20%, 40%

Left: Clicking multiple times samples isolated areas.
Middle: Clicking and dragging in an "L" shape samples all the colors in a rectangular area.
Right: Sampling an L-shaped area by drawing two rectangles that touch each other.

By adjusting the **Range** setting, and being careful with where you click within an image, it's often possible to isolate individual objects from scenes that contain other objects of the same color.

Original image as it appeared before attempting to make a selection using Color Range.

Result of attempting to select the triangular area at the top of the building with the Localized Color Clusters checkbox turned off. Multiple areas were clicked on and the Fuzziness was adjusted until all of the triangular area was selected (shown using Black Matte Preview setting).

Result of attempting to remove areas using the Minus Eyedropper tool.

This message was displayed after attempting to remove areas with the Minus Eyedropper tool.

Turning off the **Localized Color Clusters** checkbox after creating a selection will show you what clicking on the same areas would have produced in previous versions of Photoshop.

Original image before selection was made.

Result of clicking multiple times within the triangular area at the top of the building with the Localized Color Clusters checkbox turned on, and the Range setting at 100%.

Selection created using Localized Color Clusters shown as black overlay.

Result of reducing the Range setting to the lowest number that fully selected the triangular area.

Result of clicking with the Minus Eyedropper tool on various points within the lower region of the image until only the triangular area was selected.

Result of turning off the Localized Color Clusters checkbox after creating the selection shown above.

Available on Layer Masks

In previous versions of Photoshop, **Color Range** was only available for creating or modifying selections. In CS4 you can use **Color Range** to populate or modify a Layer Mask. All you have to do is make sure a Layer Mask is active when you choose **Select>Color Range**.

In a Layer Mask, white preserves the layer's appearance while black hides the contents of the layer. The **Color Range** dialog box is not capable of adding white to a mask, so all it can do is cause more areas to become hidden by adding black to the mask. That means that areas in a mask that were black before you applied **Color Range** will remain black regardless of what you do in the dialog box.

The areas you click on with the Eyedroppers in the **Color Range** dialog box will be preserved (along with previous content of the mask), while all other areas will turn solid black. This has the effect of hiding the areas you do not click on. If that poses a problem, and you'd rather

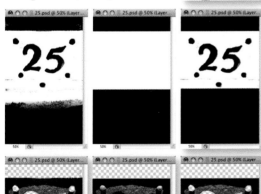

The image at top is the original. The middle row shows masks that produce the results shown below them. From left to right: Mask made by Color Range. A hand-made mask. The result of starting with the hand-made mask and using Color Range to refine it.

hide the areas you click on and keep the areas you don't, just turn on the **Invert** checkbox on the right side of the dialog box.

If a selection is active at the time you choose **Color Range** and a **Layer Mask** is also active, the selection will limit where the mask can be modified.

I find this new ability to create and modify Layer Masks with Color Range is especially powerful when combined with the new **Adjustments** panel. Here's a typical workflow:

Original image.

Create An Adjustment: I open an image, click on one of the icons in the **Adjustments** panel (to create a new Adjustment Layer) and begin to make an adjustment only to realize that I'd like it to be restricted to a small area of the image.

Black & White Adjustment Layer added.

Limit Area: I choose **Select>Color Range** and experiment with the settings until the adjustment only affects the areas I desire.

Fine-tune Adjustment: Because I never had to commit the adjustment (it's still active in the **Adjustments** panel), I am able to continue to modify the adjustment until I like the results.

Color Range used to modify the Layer Mask.

Fine-tune Mask: Once I'm done with the adjustment, I grab the **Brush** tool and paint over various areas to fine-tune the mask until it suits my needs.

The resulting mask can be fine-tuned with any tool.

Flash Panels

With Photoshop CS4, Adobe is allowing third party developers to create their own Flash-based (SWF) panels that look just like the panels you use everyday in Photoshop. You can load most SWF format files into the **Photoshop/Plug-Ins/Panels** folder, relaunch Photoshop and then access them from the **Window>Extensions** menu.

To give you an idea of what's possible  with this newfangled kind of customization, let's take a look at the two Flash-based panels (both developed by Adobe) that are included with Photoshop CS4.

Kuler Panel

The new **Kuler** panel (**Window>Extensions>Kuler**) is a sophisticated color picker that allows you to share a collection of colors—also known as a 'theme'—with other users via Adobe Kuler (**kuler.adobe.com**), a web-based application where you can browse thousands of color themes created by the Kuler community.

The panel is divided into three sections: **1) About**, which informs you of the purpose of the **Kuler** panel, **2) Browse**, for searching the Kuler inventory of color themes, and **3) Create**, which allows you to experiment with color and create your own theme. Let's look more closely at the **Browse** and **Create** sections.

Browse

The **Browse** section allows you to access Kuler's vast inventory of color themes as well as any themes you've created yourself. The two pop-up menus determine which themes will be visible. The left pop-up menu allows you to choose between the most popular, highest rated or newest themes that are stored on-line, or access themes that you've previously saved. The right pop-up menu limits the range of results to themes that were posted in the last 7 days, 30 days, or to include all themes.

The icons at the bottom of the panel allow you to cycle through more theme sets, refresh your list with the on-line server, add the selected theme to Photoshop's **Swatches** panel, or move the theme to the **Create** section, where you can edit the theme to your liking.

KULER BROWSE ICONS	
Name	**Icon**
View Next Set	
View Previous Set	
Refresh Themes	
Edit in Create Section	
Add to Swatches	

Create

The **Create** section is where you can create or modify a theme. Selecting from the menu at the top of the panel allows you to choose between different types of color relationships. You can then use the

KULER CREATE ICONS	
Name	**Icon**
Foreground as Base	
Background as Base	
Make Active Color the Base	
Add Color to Theme	
Remove Active Color	
Add to Swatches	
Upload to Kuler Site	

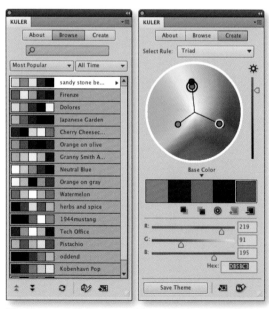

The Browse and Create sections of the Kuler panel.

icons in the panel to select the color on which you like to base the theme, add the newly created theme to Photoshop's **Swatches** panel, or upload it to Adobe Kuler to share with others.

To choose a color on which to base your theme, either click the **Foreground as Base** or **Background as Base** icons (to transfer your foreground or background color to the **Kuler** panel), or drag the circle that has a double outline within the color wheel that appears at the top of the panel.

Once you have chosen the base color, you can drag the secondary colors (indicated by a single outline) to manipulate the relationship between the colors. If you'd like to promote one of the secondary colors to the base position, click on the secondary color to make it active and then click the **Make Active Color the Base** icon.

When you're happy with the theme you've created, you have three options: **1)** click the **Save Theme** button at the bottom of the panel to save the theme so you can access it later by viewing Saved themes in the **Browse** section, **2)** click the **Add to Swatches** icon to load the theme into the **Swatches** panel so you can use the colors within Photoshop, or **3)** click the **Upload to Kuler Site** icon to share the theme with other Kuler users.

Connections Panel

This new panel is designed to allow you to interface with your AdobeID account on Adobe's web site. Adobe didn't have the back end support set up at the time of this writing, so I wasn't able to do more than look at the options available on the side menu of the panel. I've been told that you might be able to search for and download additional panels from within the **Connections** panel in the future, but it's not something I could test.

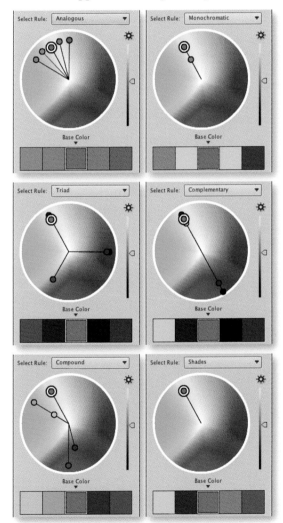

The new Connections panel in Photoshop CS4.

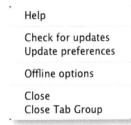

The side menu of the Connections panel.

No updates were found when I tried the Check for Updates option.

The six choices above are found in the Select Rule pop-up menu near the top of the Kuler panel, along with Custom, which allows you to create a theme that does not conform to the rules found in the pop-up menu.

Save for Web & Devices

The **Save for Web & Devices** dialog box received quite a makeover in CS4, and at first glance it seems like there should be a bunch of new features, but in fact most of the changes had to do with moving, deleting or slightly modifying existing features. Let's take a tour of what's been altered, and then we'll look at what's new.

Where's My Stuff?

When you first choose **File>Save For Web & Devices**, you might find your mouse wandering aimlessly because many of the controls have been rearranged or changed. Here's a list of what's been moved or modified:

Buttons Moved: The **Save**, **Cancel** and **Done** buttons were moved to the bottom of the dialog box and the **Device Central** button shifted from the far bottom-right to the far bottom-left edge of the dialog box.

New Side Menu Icons: A cosmetic change was made to the various side menu icons that were found on the right edge of the **Save For Web & Devices** dialog box. They've simply been updated to match the appearance of the side menus in Photoshop's various panels.

Image Size: The **Image Size** tab was un-tabbed and given its own section in the main window, just below the **Color Table**. In the process, a few changes were made. The **Original Size** readouts are gone and the **Constrain Proportions** feature can now only be accessed by clicking on the **Chain** icon that appears next to the **Width** and **Height** fields. The **Apply** button has also been removed because the new design applies the changes as soon as you press **Tab**, or click on a different field within the dialog box.

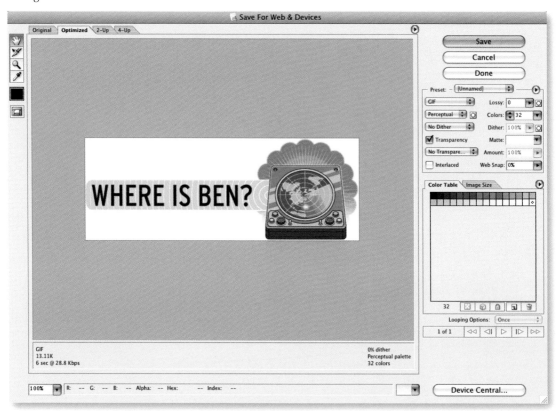

The Save For Web & Devices dialog box as found in Photoshop CS3.

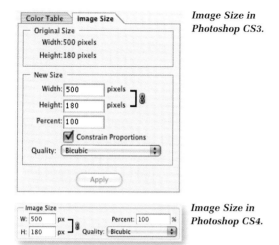

Image Size in Photoshop CS3.

The download speed setting is now found in a pop-up menu next to the download time that's listed in the lower left of the Optimized view preview area.

The **Browser Dither Options** and **Hide Auto Slices** that were found in the pop-up menu in Photoshop CS3 have disappeared and no equivalents are found in Photoshop CS4.

The color related settings have been moved to a new **Preview** pop-up menu that's found below the compression settings on the right side of the dialog box. The options available are the same, but the names have been changed in the following ways: **Uncompensated Color** has become **Monitor Color**, **Standard Windows Color** is now **Windows (No Color Management)**, **Standard Macintosh Color** is **Macintosh (No Color Management)** and **Use Document Color Profile** is simply **Use Document Profile**.

Image Size in Photoshop CS4.

Preview Menu Missing: The side menu that used to be found at the top of the preview image has been removed. The controls that used to be found in that menu are now found in various areas of the **Save for Web & Devices** dialog box.

The Save For Web & Devices dialog box as found in Photoshop CS4.

The preview options that were found in Photoshop CS3.

The new Preview pop-up menu in Photoshop CS4.

Convert to sRGB: This option has been removed from the compression side menu and has been added as a checkbox in the main compression area.

Include XMP: This item was moved from the side menu of the compression area and transformed into the new **Metadata** pop-up menu that's found in the main area of the dialog box. Switching between the **None** and **All** options is the same as toggling the old **Include XMP** option off and on. We'll discuss the new options found in the menu later in this chapter.

Channel-Based Features: The icon that allowed you to use an Alpha Channel to influence how a feature worked (such as the **Lossy** and **Dither** options) has been removed and no equivalent can be found in Photoshop CS4. This is a major loss for those of us who really wanted to squeeze our images into the smallest files possible.

Include ICC Profile: This option has simply been renamed **Embed Color Profile**. Nothing has changed other than its name.

New Features

Now don't go getting all excited by that heading. There's really not much that's been added to the **Save For Web & Devices** dialog box. You'll only find the following two new features:

Zoom Controls

They've added plus and minus icons next to the magnification setting. Clicking these icons will zoom in or out on your image by a preset amount (50%, 66.7%, 100%, 200%, etc.).

Metadata Options

The new **Metadata** pop-up menu allows you to determine how much non-image data is included with your image. Here are the choices you have:

None: Will produce the smallest file size (since no metadata will be included with the image). When this setting is active a warning triangle will appear next to the **Save** button to warn you that no copyright information will be included in the file.

Copyright: Will embed whatever info you've placed in the copyright section of the **File Info** dialog box which is found under the **File** menu. If the **Copyright Status** pop-up menu is set to **Copyrighted**, a copyright symbol (©) will appear next to the file name (if the image is opened in Photoshop).

Copyright and Contact Info: Will include copyright information (as mentioned above) along with **Author**, **Author Title** and any information that's been entered into the **IPTC Contact** section of the **File Info** dialog box.

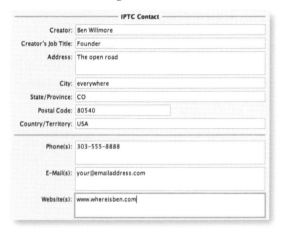

All Except Camera Info: Will embed all the information that's found in the **File Info** dialog box, with the exception of the information that's found under the **Camera Data** tab.

All: As you might have guessed, this option will include all the information that's found in the **File Info** dialog box.

Color Management

Photoshop's support for **ICC Color Profiles** has been greatly enhanced in CS4. A **Profile** is used to describe a **Color Space**, which is a set of instructions that contain information about the document's color mode (such as **RGB**, **CMYK** or **Grayscale),** along with the descriptive details needed to accurately display an image (such as the exact colors of cyan, magenta, yellow and black ink and paper color to be used in CMYK mode). Here's what they've added in CS4:

Color Blind Preview

Adobe has partnered with the University of Tokyo to come up with certified ICC profiles that are designed to simulate how a color blind person might interpret images.

In Europe and the United States, one out of every 10-12 males and one in every 200 females is believed to be color blind. As our society incorporates more color into everything (cell phones, cash machines, printed matter, etc.) life is becoming increasingly difficult for people who are color blind, so it's good to see that some serious effort is going into improving their ability to deal with color (at least digitally).

By choosing one of the options found in the **View>Proof Setup>Color Blindness** menu, you can view your image in a way that is similar to how a color blind person might see it.

There are two types of simulations available:

Protanopia: This choice simulates how an image might look to someone whose sensitivity to red light is impaired. This is the most common type of color-blindness and has the effect of causing confusion for a person trying to distinguish between greens, reds and yellows.

Deuteranopia: This choice simulates how an image might look to someone whose sensitivity to green light is impaired. This type of color-blindness also makes it difficult to distinguish between greens, reds and yellows.

Original logo design.

Modified logo design.

Logo shown above viewed with a Protanopia preview.

Modified logo viewed with a Protanopia preview.

The same image viewed with a Deuteranopia preview.

Modified logo viewed with a Deuteranopia preview.

The menu on the left shows the View menu with Proof Setup submenu:

View

Proof Setup ▶
✓ Proof Colors   ⌘Y
  Gamut Warning   ⇧⌘Y
  Pixel Aspect Ratio ▶
  Pixel Aspect Ratio Correction
  32-bit Preview Options...

  Zoom In   ⌘+
  Zoom Out   ⌘−
  Fit on Screen   ⌘0
  Actual Pixels   ⌘1
  Print Size

  Screen Mode ▶

✓ Extras   ⌘H
  Show ▶

  Rulers   ⌘R

✓ Snap   ⇧⌘;
  Snap To ▶

  Lock Guides   ⌥⌘;
  Clear Guides
  New Guide...

  Lock Slices
  Clear Slices

Proof Setup submenu:

Custom...

Working CMYK
Working Cyan Plate
Working Magenta Plate
Working Yellow Plate
Working Black Plate
Working CMY Plates

Macintosh RGB
Windows RGB
Monitor RGB

✓ Color Blindness – Protanopia-type
  Color Blindness – Deuteranopia-type

Original image.

Choosing one of the Color Blindness options will automatically turn on the Proof Colors feature to simulate what your image would look like to someone who has that type of color blindness.

Same image viewed with a Protanopia preview.

Same image viewed with a Deuteranopia preview.

When you choose one of the options mentioned above, Photoshop will automatically turn on the **Proof Colors** option that is found in the **View** menu. You can toggle the preview on and off by typing **Command-Y** (Mac), or **Ctrl-Y** (Win) which toggles the **Proof Colors** option off or on. Toggling the preview off and on can be useful when you are choosing colors for a design or adjusting an image where the color is critical to the communication of the image.

The simulations are by no means perfect, so it is best to have a color blind person evaluate your images if you're designing for that audience. The challenge here is that color blind people have a much greater ability to distinguish between different brightness and saturation levels in an image because they often have to rely on that ability to differentiate between colors. Slight differences in brightness might not be perceived by someone with unimpaired vision, while a color blind person might be able to easily distinguish the difference.

> ⎯ NOTE ⎯
>
> **Colorblind Design Resource**
>
> For more information about making images that are designed with the color blind in mind, visit the Color Universal Design web site at:
> **www.cudo.jp/e/**

Left: A critical sign design. Bottom Left: As viewed with a Protanopia preview. Bottom Right: As viewed with a Deuteranopia preview.

Revamped Convert to Profile Dialog Box

Adobe has added all sorts of new functionality to the **Convert to Profile** dialog box (which is found under the **Edit** menu).

This dialog box allows you to convert an image from one Color Space to another. Take a deep breath here because this is going to get a bit technical (unavoidably so), but I'll try to keep it as close to plain English as I can. Keep in mind that this dialog box is meant for color geeks who really know what they are doing. If that doesn't describe you, you might want to skip to the Misc. Changes section of this chapter on page 120.

A Color Space is a set of instructions that contain information about a document's color mode (such as RGB, CMYK or Grayscale) along with additional information that is needed to accurately reproduce the image (such as the exact shades of red, green and blue that are needed to define the colors that make up your RGB image). You've most likely worked with, or are at least aware of, a few basic color spaces such as **Adobe RGB** or **sRGB**.

In the past, anytime you changed between modes via the **Image>Mode** menu, the **Edit>Convert to Profile** feature was what did the actual work even though Photoshop didn't display a dialog box. Changing modes as mentioned above is the same as choosing **Working RGB**, **Working CMYK** or **Working Gray** from the **Profile** pop-up menu in the **Convert to Profile** dialog box and leaving all the other settings at their defaults. So, in essence, the **Convert to Profile** dialog box is a mechanism that allows you to convert your document from one mode to another.

But, unlike the choices found in the **Image>Mode** menu, the **Convert to Profile** dialog box is not limited to the default color spaces. With the **Convert to Profile** dialog box, you can convert between two different flavors of the same mode (such as **sRGB** and **Adobe RGB**) and a bunch more options are at your disposal which give you much greater control over the process. Let's take a look at the new features they've added in Photoshop CS4.

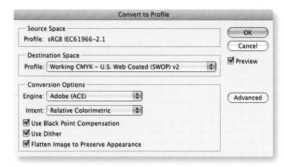

The Convert to Profile dialog box in Photoshop CS4.

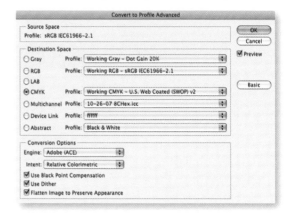

Clicking the Advanced button produces this dialog box.

There are now two versions of the dialog box. You can switch between them by clicking the **Advanced/Basic** button that's found just below the **Preview** checkbox. The Basic version is mostly the same as it was in previous releases of Photoshop, so we'll just skip that one, and move on to exploring the Advanced version.

The choices that are found in the **Profile** pop-up menu of the Advanced version are grouped into seven categories. The top four categories contain the choices that were available in previous versions of Photoshop, but they've been reorganized based on the mode they represent (Gray, RGB, CMYK, etc.). That makes finding the color space you desire much easier than having to search for it in the overly lengthy menu from the Basic version (which is why I never use the Basic version of the dialog box).

Working RGB – sRGB IEC61966-2.1
✓ Working CMYK – U.S. Web Coated (SWOP) v2
Working Gray – Dot Gain 20%

Lab Color

Custom RGB...
Custom CMYK...
Custom Dot Gain...
Custom Gamma...

Other

Adobe RGB (1998)
Apple RGB
ColorMatch RGB
ProPhoto RGB
sRGB IEC61966-2.1

Coated FOGRA27 (ISO 12647-2:2004)
Coated FOGRA39 (ISO 12647-2:2004)
Coated GRACoL 2006 (ISO 12647-2:2004)
Japan Color 2001 Coated
Japan Color 2001 Uncoated
Japan Color 2002 Newspaper
Japan Color 2003 Web Coated
Japan Web Coated (Ad)
U.S. Sheetfed Coated v2
U.S. Sheetfed Uncoated v2
U.S. Web Coated (SWOP) v2
U.S. Web Uncoated v2
Uncoated FOGRA29 (ISO 12647-2:2004)
Web Coated FOGRA28 (ISO 12647-2:2004)
Web Coated SWOP 2006 Grade 3 Paper
Web Coated SWOP 2006 Grade 5 Paper

Dot Gain 10%
Dot Gain 15%
Dot Gain 20%
Dot Gain 25%
Dot Gain 30%
Gray Gamma 1.8
Gray Gamma 2.2

7-18-08 Monitor Profile 100
7-18-08 Monitor Profile 120 Lum
ARRIFLEX D-20 Daylight Log (by Adobe)
ARRIFLEX D-20 Tungsten Log (by Adobe)
Camera RGB Profile
CIE RGB
Cinema HD
Color LCD
Dalsa Origin Tungsten Lin (by Adobe)
e-sRGB
Fujifilm ETERNA 250 Printing Density (by Adobe)
Fujifilm ETERNA 250D Printing Density (by Adobe)
Fujifilm ETERNA 400 Printing Density (by Adobe)
Fujifilm ETERNA 500 Printing Density (by Adobe)
Fujifilm F-125 Printing Density (by Adobe)
Fujifilm F-64D Printing Density (by Adobe)
Fujifilm REALA 500D Printing Density (by Adobe)
Generic RGB Profile
HDTV (Rec. 709)
Kodak 5205/7205 Printing Density (by Adobe)
Kodak 5218/7218 Printing Density (by Adobe)
Kodak 5229/7229 Printing Density (by Adobe)
NTSC (1953)
PAL/SECAM
Panavision Genesis Tungsten Log (by Adobe)
Pro38 ARMP
Pro38 EMP
Pro38 PGPP
Pro38 PLPP
Pro38 PPSmC
Pro38 PQUP_MK
Pro38 PSPP
Pro38 SWMP
Pro38 SWMP_LD
Pro38 USFAP
Pro38 VFAP
Pro38 WCRW
Pro3800 3800C 3850 Standard
ROMM-RGB
SDTV NTSC
SDTV PAL
SMPTE-C
SP3800_EFP_PK_2880
Viper FilmStream Daylight Log (by Adobe)
Viper FilmStream Tungsten Log (by Adobe)
Wide Gamut RGB

Euroscale Coated v2
Euroscale Uncoated v2
Generic CMYK Profile
Photoshop 4 Default CMYK
Photoshop 5 Default CMYK

Generic Gray Profile
sGray

The Profile menu in the Basic version of the Convert to Profile dialog box. I've wasted too much of my life trying to find the three or four profiles I use from this overly long menu.

Note: I have some 3rd party profiles installed that do not come with Photoshop. They are the profiles that start with Pro38 and are profiles for an Epson 3800 printer.

✓ Working Gray – Dot Gain 20%
Custom Dot Gain...
Custom Gamma...
Other

Dot Gain 10%
Dot Gain 15%
Dot Gain 20%
Dot Gain 25%
Dot Gain 30%
Gray Gamma 1.8
Gray Gamma 2.2

Generic Gray Profile
sGray

The Gray pop-up menu in the Advanced version of the dialog box makes it easy to find grayscale profiles.

✓ Working RGB – sRGB IEC61966-2.1
Custom RGB...

Adobe RGB (1998)
Apple RGB
ColorMatch RGB
ProPhoto RGB
sRGB IEC61966-2.1

7-18-08 Monitor Profile 100
7-18-08 Monitor Profile 120 Lum
ARRIFLEX D-20 Daylight Log (by Adobe)
ARRIFLEX D-20 Tungsten Log (by Adobe)
Camera RGB Profile
CIE RGB
Cinema HD
Color LCD
Dalsa Origin Tungsten Lin (by Adobe)
e-sRGB
Fujifilm ETERNA 250 Printing Density (by Adobe)
Fujifilm ETERNA 250D Printing Density (by Adobe)
Fujifilm ETERNA 400 Printing Density (by Adobe)
Fujifilm ETERNA 500 Printing Density (by Adobe)
Fujifilm F-125 Printing Density (by Adobe)
Fujifilm F-64D Printing Density (by Adobe)
Fujifilm REALA 500D Printing Density (by Adobe)
Generic RGB Profile
HDTV (Rec. 709)
Kodak 5205/7205 Printing Density (by Adobe)
Kodak 5218/7218 Printing Density (by Adobe)
Kodak 5229/7229 Printing Density (by Adobe)
NTSC (1953)
PAL/SECAM
Panavision Genesis Tungsten Log (by Adobe)
Pro38 ARMP
Pro38 EMP
Pro38 PGPP
Pro38 PLPP
Pro38 PPSmC
Pro38 PQUP_MK
Pro38 PSPP
Pro38 SWMP
Pro38 SWMP_LD
Pro38 USFAP
Pro38 VFAP
Pro38 WCRW
Pro3800 3800C 3850 Standard
ROMM-RGB
SDTV NTSC
SDTV PAL
SMPTE-C
SP3800_EFP_PK_2880
Viper FilmStream Daylight Log (by Adobe)
Viper FilmStream Tungsten Log (by Adobe)
Wide Gamut RGB

The RGB pop-up menu in the Advanced version of the dialog box makes it easy to find RGB profiles.

Note: Many desktop printers are listed in the RGB menu even though they reproduce images using CMYK inks. That's because Photoshop sends those devices RGB information and the printer driver handles the conversion to CMYK after the image leaves Photoshop's control.

✓ Working CMYK – U.S. Web Coated (SWOP) v2
Custom CMYK...
Other

Coated FOGRA27 (ISO 12647-2:2004)
Coated FOGRA39 (ISO 12647-2:2004)
Coated GRACoL 2006 (ISO 12647-2:2004)
Japan Color 2001 Coated
Japan Color 2001 Uncoated
Japan Color 2002 Newspaper
Japan Color 2003 Web Coated
Japan Web Coated (Ad)
U.S. Sheetfed Coated v2
U.S. Sheetfed Uncoated v2
U.S. Web Coated (SWOP) v2
U.S. Web Uncoated v2
Uncoated FOGRA29 (ISO 12647-2:2004)
Web Coated FOGRA28 (ISO 12647-2:2004)
Web Coated SWOP 2006 Grade 3 Paper
Web Coated SWOP 2006 Grade 5 Paper

Euroscale Coated v2
Euroscale Uncoated v2
Generic CMYK Profile
Photoshop 4 Default CMYK
Photoshop 5 Default CMYK

The CMYK pop-up menu in the Advanced version of the dialog box makes it easy to find CMYK profiles.

Linked Profile Support

The new **Device Link** pop-up menu allows you to use linked profiles to convert between two flavors of the same mode (like **U.S. Sheetfed Coated** and **U.S. Web Uncoated**, which are both flavors of **CMYK** mode). A linked profile is one that contains a direct link between two color spaces without needing to use **Lab** mode as a conversion space. Linked profiles are primarily used to convert between different flavors of **CMYK** mode.

You have to use specialized software to create linked profiles and none of them ship with Photoshop, so most users will be unable to experiment with this feature.

I use a product called **Link-o-lator** from **LeftDakota.com** to produce linked profiles. With that product you can perform special tasks such as making sure registration marks maintain their 100% cyan, 100% magenta, 100% yellow, 100% black mixture—even after converting to a different CMYK color space—and making sure black-only text does not get contaminated by other inks in the process.

Linked profiles are primarily of interest for pre-press professionals who really know their stuff. The software I use to create them costs almost $2000.

There's one noticeable problem with Photoshop CS4's implementation of linked profiles—the resulting image is not tagged with the destination color profile. That means if you convert an image

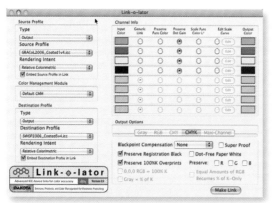

Some of the controls available in Left Dakota's Link-o-lator application for creating linked profiles.

from **U.S. Sheetfed Coated** to **U.S. Web Uncoated**, it will still be tagged as a **U.S. Sheetfed Coated** file. To tag the file correctly, be sure you choose **Edit>Assign Profile** and assign the profile of the color space you've converted into.

Adobe has been trying to follow the standards set forth by the International Color Consortium (also known as the ICC), but they have not come up with a method for including the source and destination profiles in a linked profile. Adobe wasn't able to tag the image with the proper profile because the linked profiles do not contain the information needed. The Link-o-lator product is capable of embedding both the source and destination profiles into a linked profile, but the method used has not been endorsed by the ICC and therefore Adobe didn't take advantage of it.

Spot Color Profile Support

The new **Multichannel** pop-up menu allows you to take advantage of profiles that are designed to separate an image into a maximum of sixteen spot colors. Photoshop does not ship with any multichannel profiles, so this menu will be empty unless you create and install a custom profile.

Multichannel profiles can be created by products such as **X-rite's Monaco Profiler Platinum** which is a $4,000+ software package for creating profiles with up to 8 colors, or **GretagMacbeth's Profile-maker Packaging**, which costs over $10,000 and can produce profiles for up to 10 colors.

Multichannel profiles are primarily used in the packaging and T-shirt printing industry where images are often reproduced using spot colors.

When using a multichannel profile in the **Convert to Profile** dialog box, completely ignore the on-screen preview that is displayed because the technology used for producing in-dialog-box-previews is not capable of producing previews of more than four colors.

The names of the channels that you end up with are determined by the profile that was used. Some profiles use generic names like "Colorant 1." If you're using a profile that doesn't label the chan-

Original image as it looked before being converted to seven colors using a multichannel profile.

The result of converting the image at left using a seven color multichannel profile.

nels, consider double-clicking on each channel and renaming them to reflect the Pantone colors you plan to print with.

The on-screen appearance of the image after you leave the **Convert to Profile** dialog box should be treated as an approximation of what the image will look like when printed. That's because it is using a rather crude spot color compositing engine from previous versions of Photoshop. This might sound like a huge limitation, but most people who work with spot color separations are not used to getting an accurate on-screen preview anyway. This new support is a very welcome change and can produce some great looking printed images. We can only hope Adobe invests the time needed to figure out how to produce a more accurate composite image in a future version of Photoshop.

Abstract Profile Support

Adobe engineers didn't stop after adding support for the profile types that advanced prepress users were clamoring for. In CS4 you can also use an obscure type of profile that's known as an Abstract Profile.

I don't know of a single piece of software that is capable of producing an Abstract Profile. They are primarily created by color scientists doing research on color profiles. *Mac OSX's profiles.*

An Abstract Profile converts an image within its own color space while applying a visual change to the image. Photoshop does not ship with any of these profiles, but Apple has included five of them with the Mac operating system.

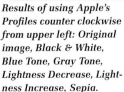

Results of using Apple's Profiles counter clockwise from upper left: Original image, Black & White, Blue Tone, Gray Tone, Lightness Decrease, Lightness Increase, Sepia.

Scene-referred Profile Support

A new option has been added to the **Color Settings** dialog box (accessed via the **Edit** menu). Turning on the **Compensate for Scene-referred Profiles** checkbox can help to produce a more consistent color match between the view of an image in Photoshop and Adobe After Effects.

Graphics designers and photographers don't have to worry about this setting because it only applies to images that utilize scene-referred profiles.

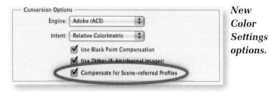

New Color Settings options.

Misc. Changes

This next bunch of tweaks are not immediately obvious, but many are worth knowing about, so don't stop reading here.

64-Bit Native on Windows:

Photoshop CS4 can run in 64-bit mode when installed under Windows Vista 64 running under a 64-bit processor. 64-bit mode allows Photoshop to access more than 4GB of memory, which can be a big help when working on huge multi-layered images.

It's not overly practical to run Photoshop in 64-bit mode if you're using a laptop computer because most laptops are limited to 4GB of memory. Without the advantage of additional memory, laptop users can expect around a 10% speed boost when running Photoshop in 64-bit mode.

64-bit support is not available on the Mac because Apple made a surprise announcement during their World Wide Developers Conference that they were canceling their plans to offer 64-bit support for applications written in their Carbon development environment. That means projects have to be ported to something known as Cocoa in order to run natively in 64-bit mode. Because of Apple's unexpected about-face, Adobe has to come up with a bunch of workarounds to get

Photoshop to be 64-bit native on the Mac platform. Adobe could have done it with CS4, but they would have had to reduce the feature set in order to devote enough engineers to the task.

If you work with massive files, you might consider transitioning to Windows in order to gain access to more than 4GB of RAM. If you're a Mac user who works on multi-gigabyte images and your computer is running an Intel processor, you should be able to purchase a copy of Windows and install it on your machine through Apple's Bootcamp application.

Print Options

Multiple changes have been made in the **Print** dialog box (which is accessed via the **File** menu). Let's take a look at each change, one at a time:

Gamut Warning: This new checkbox is found directly below the preview on the left side of the **Print** dialog box and is only available if you have the **Color Handling** pop-up menu set to **Photoshop Manages Colors**. Turning this option on will display gray over any parts of your image that are more colorful than your output device can reproduce. Those are areas that will change appearance when you print the file. The only problem with this new feature is that it does not indicate how much color shift will occur, only that it will occur, so you don't get enough information to know if the shift in color will be acceptable or objectionable.

Left: Original image. Right: The same image shown with the Gamut Warning option active.

If you'd like to see what will happen to those colors when the image is printed, turn on the **Match Print Colors** checkbox to get a preview of the final output. With that option turned on, the colors that are unprintable will shift on-screen to show you what they'll look like when printed.

Show Paper White: When this checkbox is turned off, Photoshop displays white areas of your image as being bright white in the preview. Turning this option on will cause the image to darken to simulate what it would look like when printed on the paper that is specified in the profile you've chosen under the **Printer Profile** pop-up menu on the right side of the **Print** dialog box. Almost all papers are darker than the white of your monitor, so this option can help to get the on-screen preview to better match your printed results.

16-bit Output: A new checkbox was added to the **Output** section of the **Print** dialog box (accessed via the pop-up menu near the top right of the dialog box). Turning on the **Send 16-bit Data** checkbox will cause Photoshop to send up to 16-bits of data per channel to your printer. That means thousands of brightness levels will be used to print your image, instead of the standard 256 (also known as 8-bit) that has been available in previous versions of Photoshop.

Sending more information to your printer has the potential of producing smoother transitions and less banding, but might have the consequence of slowing down the print job because the printer has to process twice as much data (16-bit files take up twice as much space as 8-bit files on your hard drive). Using this checkbox is only an advantage if your image is currently in 16-bit mode and actually contains more than 8-bits of information.

Left: Shown with Show Paper White turned off. Right: The same image with Show Paper White turned on.

The Print dialog box as it appears in Photoshop CS4.

Missing Output Options: Adobe has removed the **Screen** and **Transfer** options that were found in the Output section of the Photoshop CS3 **Print** dialog box, and has not provided any alternatives.

Tiny Changes: They've added a paper size readout above the preview to remind you of the settings you've specified in the **Page Setup** dialog box. It may be a tiny change, but it's a welcome one since I can't even count the number of times I've tried to print with the wrong page size selected.

Tiny Tweaks

Okay, we're down to the truly miniscule stuff that few would notice if it weren't pointed out.

Revised File Info dialog box: Adobe changed the layout and added options to the **File Info** dialog box which is accessed via the **File** menu. We covered those changes in the chapter on Bridge, but I'm mentioning it here just in case you skipped that chapter.

Share My Screen: A new option has been added to the **File** menu that allows you to share your screen with up to three other users. The technology behind this option is not new; it's simply using Adobe's Acrobat Connect service, which you can use from any web browser. A similar feature was added to Bridge in Photoshop CS3.

Edit in QuickMask Mode: If you hate working with icons—because you can't remember which icon refers to which feature—you'll be very happy to know that you can now enter Quick Mask Mode by choosing **Edit in Quick Mask Mode** from the **Select** menu, instead of clicking on the Quick Mask icon at the bottom of the Tool bar.

Cache Levels Changed: Adobe snuck in and changed the default **Cache Levels** setting from 6 to 4 in the **Performance** section of Photoshop's **Preferences** dialog box. I really doubt you'll notice much of a performance change, but it might save a little bit of memory in the process, especially when working with overly high resolution images.

The Output settings in Photoshop CS3.

The Output settings in Photoshop CS4.

Keep in Touch

Anyone who has been around Photoshop for more than two minutes knows that this is an application with a daunting arsenal of tools. CS4 added another level of power and complexity, making the learning curve a few inches longer. Many features are relatively straightforward and easy to grasp, while others can present a bit of an obstacle course. Sometimes the biggest challenge is simply knowing which tool to use! That's why learning Photoshop is a life-long pursuit for any-one serious about mastering its full potential.

Books are essential ingredients in the stew of resources necessary to keep us functioning as Photoshop superheroes, but there is an entire universe of other resources out there that will do wonders to support your personal evolution with digital imaging. My part of that universe is avail-able through my web site, **DigitalMastery.com**, my blog, **WhereisBen.com**, and my photography site, **TheBestofBen.com.**

At **DigitalMastery.com** you'll find my seminar/ conference schedule, books and DVDs, as well a bunch of free resources including my magazine articles, tips and tutorials.

At **WhereisBen.com** you'll find my travel diary (destinations range from Dubai, Russia, and Ice-land to places as obscure as Kerrville, Texas), more magazine articles, radio interviews, and just about anything I find interesting.

At **TheBestofBen.com** you can explore examples of the photographs I've taken recently.

I encourage you to visit my sites, and I'd love to see you at one my events, or hear from you if you have something to say that you feel would make this a better book. Just write to me at **book@digitalmastery.com**. I don't get around to answering every message, but I do read them all.

Best of luck to you as you wrap yourself around CS4. I hope this book gives you what you need as you launch yourself toward Photoshop nirvana!

Index

Symbols & Numerics

+ (plus) icon on Eyedropper tool, 103, 105
- (minus) icon on Eyedropper tool, 103, 106
16-bit output to printer, 121
64-bit mode in Windows, 120

A

Abstract Profiles, 119
ACR (Adobe Camera Raw). See Camera Raw 5.0
Actual Pixels command, 71
Add Mask icons, 94
Adjustment Brush (Camera Raw), 28–33
  adjusting color, 31
  brush setting features, 28–30
  Clarity slider of, 36
  overview, 27, 37
  slider settings for, 31
  using pins, 32
adjustment icons, 51, 53
Adjustment Layers.
  See also Adjustments panel
  keyboard shortcuts for, 50, 59
  major interface changes, 49–50
  using Masks panel with, 55

adjustments
  avoiding saturation clipping with Vibrance, 49, 55–57
  feature overview for, 49, 59
  features affected by upgrade, 49–50
  miscellaneous changes, 49, 59
  Targeted Adjustment icon, 49, 58
Adjustments panel, 50–55
  combining Layer Mask with Color Range and, 107
  controls activated for, 54–55
  creating presets from, 50, 54, 59
  illustrated, 51
  modal adjustments, 51, 52–53
  overview, 49
  presets for, 50, 54, 59
Adobe Photo Downloader, 7
Alpha Channel, 77–79
Amount setting (Content-Aware Scaling feature), 76
Animated Zoom, 69
Appearance section (Web Gallery), 19
Application Bar (Photoshop), 39, 42–43
Application Frame
  about, 39, 45–46
  toggle unavailable with, 42
Apply Mask icon, 97
Arbitrary collections, 16
Arrange Documents menu, 43
Audio Annotations tool, 61, 67

Audio Data tab (File Info dialog box), 10–11
Auto button (Camera Raw), 36
Auto option (Auto-Align Layers dialog box), 80
Auto-Align Layers command, 80–83
  Collage option, 80
  fisheye corrections, 80, 82
  Geometric Distortion option, 83
  overview, 75
  panoramas using, 80, 82, 83
  Spherical option, 80
  using Photomerge with, 89
  using w/Auto-Blend Layers, 83
  Vignette Removal option, 83
Auto-Blend Layers command, 83–88
  Blend Method options, 83, 86
  overview, 75
  past versions of, 83
  Seamless Tones and Colors option, 83, 87–88, 89
  using Photomerge with, 89
  using with Auto-Align Layers, 83
auto-show hidden panels, 46
Auto-Stack Panorama/HDR command, 22–23

B

background color for full screen settings, 46
backwards compatibility for Camera Raw, 37
bars
Application, 39, 42–43
Path, 3, 15
using, 41
Batch Rename command, 7, 9
Bird's Eye View, 69
Black & White Adjustment panel, 58
black matte previews, 103
Blend Images Together checkbox (Photomerge dialog box), 81, 82, 89
blending layers automatically, 75, 83–88
Bridge CS4
changes to Photo Downloader, 7
Collections panel for, 3, 16, 24
gesture support for Macs, 24
icon in Photoshop for, 39
interface changes to, 5, 6–14
miscellaneous changes in, 20–24
moved or changed features in, 3–4
Open in Camera Raw icon, 13, 28, 36
Output panel, 3, 17–20, 24
overview, 3, 24
Path bar for, 3, 15
Review mode for, 7–9, 20
revised View options, 20
Browse section (Kuler panel), 108
brushes
drag-resizing, 62, 63
enhanced cursors for, 62
fine-tuning Layer Mask adjustments with, 107
setting diameter of, 62, 63
settings for Camera Raw images, 28–30
time savings with, 61, 62–63
Brushes panel, 62–63
Brushes Presets panel, 63
Burn tool changes, 66–67

C

caching
Bridge preferences for, 21
levels for, 122
calendar icon, 11
Camera Data tab (Save for Web & Devices dialog box), 113
camera profiles, 37
Camera Raw 5.0
Adjustment Brush in, 27, 28–33, 37
backwards compatibility of, 37
changes with upgrade to, 27
Graduated Filter in, 27, 33–34
improvements in, 27, 36–37
opening Bridge files in, 13, 28, 36
overview, 27
Post Crop Vignetting settings, 27, 34–35, 37
Change Layer Content command, 75
Channels shortcut changes, 50, 59
Clarity slider (Camera Raw), 36
Clone preview cursor, 64–65
closing tabs, 42
CMYK profiles, 116, 117
Collage option
Auto-Align Layers dialog box, 80
Photomerge dialog box, 81
collapsing
panels, 40, 42
tab groups, 41, 42
collections
defined, 16
processing in Photoshop, 23
Reveal Files feature and, 6
Smart, 16
Collections panel (Bridge), 3, 16, 24

color. See also color management
adjusting Camera Raw brush, 31
Localized Color Clusters feature, 102, 103, 104–106
preventing saturation clipping of, 56–57
previewing brush, 62
setting background for full screen settings, 46
Stroke Layer Effects default, 99
working with in Kuler panels, 101, 108–109
color management, 113–120
changes to Convert to Profile dialog box, 116–119
color blindness previews, 113–115
feature overview for, 101
gamut warnings, 120
using linked profiles, 118
Color Palette section (Web Gallery), 18–19
Color Picker dialog box, 30, 31
Color Range dialog box, 102–107
button on Masks panel for, 96
Localized Color Clusters feature of, 102, 103, 104–106
modifying Layer Mask on, 107
performance in earlier versions, 102–104
revisions to, 101, 102
Color Settings dialog box, 120
color spaces
converting images to other, 116
describing with profiles, 113
profiles linking, 118
Color Universal Design web site, 115
comments with Notes tool, 67–68
computer platforms. See Mac computers; Windows computers

K

keyboard shortcuts
Actual Pixels command, 71
Adjustment Layer, 50, 59
spring-loaded, 61, 72
Kuler extension
about, 46
panel for, 101, 108–109

L

language preference, 46
Layer Masks
adjusting density settings for, 94–95
destructive transformations for, 91
dialog box, 94
feathering, 95
inverting, 96
linking Smart Object to, 90–93, 99
modifying in Color Range dialog box, 107
layers
auto-aligning, 75, 80–83
auto-blending, 75, 83–88
changed or missing features for, 75
Content-Aware Scaling and, 75, 76–79
default change for stroke layer effect, 99
enhancements to masks, 94–98
linking Smart Object to Layer Masks, 99
loading images into, 24
miscellaneous changes to, 75, 98–99
modifying from Adjustments panel, 50–51
panoramas produced with Auto-Blend Layers, 83, 86
producing panoramas with Photomerge, 75, 84–85, 89
scripts added for, 98–99
Smart Objects, 75, 90–93

Layout settings (PDF Photo Gallery), 17
legacy behavior for Color Range dialog box, 102–104
Legacy Serial Number, 101
Lens Corrections panel (Camera Raw), 34–35
Lightroom 2.0, 37
linked profiles, 118
Link-o-lator, 118
Load As Selection icon, 97
Load Files Into Layers command (Bridge), 24
Load Files Into Stack, 89
loading
images into layers, 24
mask-based selections, 97
preventing Output panel, 20
Localized Color Clusters feature
turning off, 105, 106
using, 102, 103
Lock Thumbnail Grid icon (Bridge), 14

M

Mac computers
64-bit mode unavailable for, 120
Abstract Profiles, 119
Application bar behavior on, 42–43
changes to Channels shortcuts, 50, 59
gesture support for, 24, 71
getting used to Application Frame, 45–46
manual panorama stitching, 75
"marching ants" modified, 72
masks. See also Layer Masks; Masks panel
Context-Aware Scaling with Protection, 77–79
disabling, 98
flattening all, 98
inverting, 96
producing selection based on active, 97
shortcut for applying, 97
using Adjustment Brush, 29–31

Masks panel, 94–98
about, 75, 94
adjusting density settings from, 94–95
feathering Layer Masks with, 95
mask thumbnail on, 94
refining mask edge, 96
using with Adjustment Layers, 55
Metadata pop-up menu (Save for Web & Devices dialog box), 112
minimizing panels, 41
minus (-) icon on Eyedropper tool, 103, 106
miscellaneous changes
affecting adjustments, 49, 59
Bridge CS4, 20–24
Camera Raw 5.0, 27, 36–37
improving Photoshop CS4, 101, 120–122
Photoshop interface changes, 39, 46–47
related to layers, 75, 98–99
tools, 72–73
mixing parametric and destructive edits, 91
Mobile SWF tab (File Info dialog box), 10, 12
modal adjustments, 51, 52–53
moved or changed features
Adjustment Layers, 49–50
Bridge CS4, 3–4
Camera Raw 5.0, 27
from CS3, 101
for layers, 75
Save for Web & Devices dialog box, 110–113
tools, 61
Multichannel pop-up menu (Convert to Profile dialog box), 118–119
multiple sample points, 102–103
multi-window control, 43

menus in Advanced version of
Convert to Profile, 117

spot color, 118–119

third-party products
supporting, 118

**Proof Colors options (View
menu), 115**

**protanopia color blindness,
113–115**

Protect Skin Tones icon, 77

Protection Masks, 77–79

Quick Mask mode

editing in, 122

previewing selection as if in,
103

**quick navigation icons
(Bridge), 6–7**

R

**Range option (Color Range
dialog box), 104–105**

recent documents, 6

**Recents pop-up menu
(Bridge), 6–7**

Refine Mask dialog box, 96

**Refine pop-up menu
(Bridge), 7–12**

refining mask edge, 96

Replace Contents command, 93

repositioning tabs, 42

**resetting Smart Object
transformations, 92**

resizing brushes, 63

**restoring PDF notes to layered
file, 68**

retouching tools, 64–67

Dodge and Burn, 66–67

preview cursors for Clone and
Heal, 64–65

Vibrance sponge feature, 65

re-transforming mixed edits, 91

Reveal Files feature (Bridge), 6

Review mode (Bridge), 7–9, 20

RGB profiles, 116, 117

Rotate View tool, 61, 68

S

sample points, 102–103

saturation clipping, 56

**Saturation slider (Adjustments
panel), 55–56, 57**

**Save for Web & Devices dialog
box, 110–113**

copyright and contact info
found in, 113

Copyright Status pop-up menu,
112

features changed or missing,
110–112

illustrated, 111

Metadata pop-up menu, 112

new features of, 112–113

zoom controls in, 112

scene-referred profiles, 120

screen mode icons, 39

scripts

Flatten All Layer Effects,
98–99

Flatten All Masks, 98

scrolling, 71

scrubbing through stacks, 23

**Seamless Tones and Colors
option (Auto-Blend Layers
dialog box), 83, 87–88, 89**

Search field (Bridge), 13

selections

effect of Localized Color
Clusters on color, 104

inverting color range, 104

"marching ants" modified for,
72

mask-based, 97

previewing in Color Range
dialog box, 103

**Send 16-bit Data checkbox
(Print dialog box), 121**

**sharing screen with other users,
122**

**Show Paper White checkbox
(Print dialog box), 121**

single sample points, 102–103

**Site Info section (Web Gallery),
18**

Smart Collections, 16

Smart Objects, 90–93

converting layers to, 90, 93

implementation in CS2, 90

improvements to, 75, 90–93

linking to Layer Masks,
90–93, 99

mixing parametric and
destructive edits, 91

parametric transformations
of, 91

using Distort and Perspective
transformations with, 93

warping linked, 92

Sort pop-up menu (Path bar), 15

**Spherical option (Auto-Align
Layers dialog box), 80**

**Sponge tool with Vibrance,
65–66**

spot color profiles, 118–119

**spot removal opacity
(Camera Raw), 36**

**spring-loaded keyboard
shortcuts, 61, 72**

sRGB profiles

about, 116

converting to, 112

**Stack Images option (Auto-
Blend Layers command),
86–87**

stacks

analyzing metadata from
image, 22–23

changes in Bridge CS4, 21–23

processing collections in
Photoshop, 23

scrubbing through large, 23

working with, 21–22

**Stroke Layer Effects default
color, 99**

CATCH BEN

AT

DIGITALMASTERY.COM

and get ready to say, "Aha! I finally GET Photoshop!"